Multiple Choice Questions in Advanced Level Economics

New edition
with answers

GW00320366

ALAN J. BAKER

Lecturer in Economics
University of Leicester

Test Development and Research Unit
Objective Test Series

General Editor
John S. Hamilton

The right of the
University of Cambridge
to print and sell
all manner of books
was granted by
Henry VIII in 1534.
The University has printed
and published continuously
since 1584.

CAMBRIDGE UNIVERSITY PRESS

Cambridge
New York   New Rochelle
Melbourne   Sydney

Other books in this series
Multiple Choice Questions in French (Students' Book, Teachers' Guide and Tapes)
Common Core Advanced Level Physics Multiple Choice Questions
Multiple Choice Questions in Advanced Level Chemistry

Published by the Press Syndicate of the University of Cambridge
The Pitt Building, Trumpington Street, Cambridge CB2 1RP
32 East 57th Street, New York, NY 10022, USA
10 Stamford Road, Oakleigh, Melbourne 3166, Australia

on behalf of the Northern Ireland G.C.E. Examinations Board, the
Oxford and Cambridge Schools Examination Board, the Oxford
Delegacy of Local Examinations, the University of Cambridge Local
Examinations Syndicate, the Welsh Joint Education Committee and
the Test Development and Research Unit of the three G.C.E. boards
associated with the Universities of Oxford and Cambridge

First published 1981
New edition with answers 1985
Reprinted 1987, 1989

Printed in Great Britain at the
University Press, Cambridge

Library of Congress catalogue card number: 81-9922

ISBN 0 521 31286 8

Contents

Contents

Introduction

All of the questions in this book have been used in Advanced Level G.C.E. or Higher School Certificate examinations. They have been chosen to give you an accurate picture of the general standard of the examination and the skills you will be required to exercise. In the first part of the book each section of the syllabus is represented by either one or two ten-item tests, depending on the importance of that section in the multiple choice examination. Where two tests are included, the first will be found somewhat easier than the second, though not necessarily on completely diffent topics.

The second part of this book consists of two forty-item tests dealing, respectively, with microeconomic and macroeconomic themes. These should not be attempted until the relevant syllabus sections have all been studied and the related ten-item tests completed. It is obviously impossible to include a question on every possible topic in every section of the syllabus, but the number of questions on any syllabus section in the book as a whole is very much greater than in any one multiple choice examination.

Apart from their direct value in preparing you to take a multiple choice examination, the tests in this book can be helpful in developing your understanding of Economics. An incorrect response to a specific question may indicate a more general weakness in your understanding of the principles or knowledge being tested, and a realisation of this weakness will help you to allocate your study time effectively. It is true that a proficiency in answering multiple choice questions is hardly a worthwhile end in itself, and one important skill that is not tested in a multiple choice examination is that of developing a logical argument in essay form. However, the skills of recognising and applying relevant principles and tools of analysis are as important in essay writing as in answering multiple choice questions, and the confidence you gain through experience in the latter discipline should serve you well in the former.

A good multiple choice question is one which compels you to consider carefully each of the options presented to you before making your choice, and you should adopt the practice of reading through the full set of options before committing yourself to any one. Even under examination conditions, you should have sufficient time to follow this approach, and by doing so you will ensure that whatever mistakes you make are not simply the result of accepting the first plausible-sounding option you encounter.

Alan J. Baker

2 EXERCISES

Exercise 1 The central problem of economic societies

1 The fundamental economic problem of any society is that
   A available resources are insufficient to meet all wants.
   B there are limits to the economies of scale.
   C prices differ from opportunity costs.
   D population grows faster than output.
   E resource allocation is not optimal.

2 A fundamental distinction between planned economies and market economies is that in planned economies
   A there is great emphasis upon consumer sovereignty.
   B there is control of profits in private manufacturing industry.
   C managers are the ultimate decision-takers.
   D directives, rather than prices, are the main mechanism for allocating resources.
   E monopoly and monopsony elements are removed from the process of factor price determination.

3 Which one of the questions below **cannot** be studied by the method of positive economic analysis?
   A What goods and services are produced?
   B How are goods and services produced?
   C Is consumption a function of wealth as well as of income?
   D How should goods and services be shared out between individuals?
   E How is the level of investment determined?

4 An economy can be described as efficient in terms of production if
   A it is not dependent on imports.
   B it cannot produce more of one good without producing less of another.
   C resources are allocated exclusively by the market mechanism.
   D measured Gross National Product grows continually.
   E it allocates resources to the production of capital goods.

5   The diagram below shows the production possibilities available to a closed economy without foreign trade.

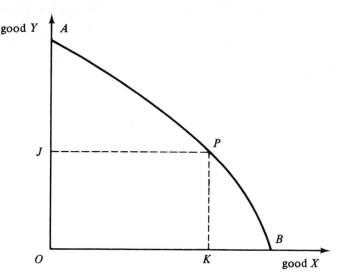

If the economy produces *OK* of good *X* then it foregoes
A   *OJ* of good *Y*.
B   *OA* of good *Y*.
C   *AJ* of good *Y*.
D   *KB* of good *X* for *OA* of good *Y*.
E   *KB* of good *X* for *AJ* of good *Y*.

6   Which one of the following could **not** be provided by means of a competitive market?
A   a health service
B   an education service
C   a fire service
D   a postal service
E   a defence service

7   Resources are efficiently allocated when
A   the rate of growth of Gross National Product is maximised.
B   production processes use the technically most efficient methods.
C   no one can be better off without someone being worse off.
D   the marginal product of capital is maximised.
E   the hours of work required to produce the national output are minimised.

4 EXERCISES

8 Assume that there are only two goods produced in a simple society, fish and meat, and that there are ten thousand man-hours available per year. It takes 50 man-hours to catch 100 kilograms of fish and 100 man-hours to raise 100 kilograms of meat. The invention of an improved fishing technique doubles productivity in the fishing industry. Which one of the following five diagrams represents the production possibility frontiers prior to the invention (P) and following the invention (F)?

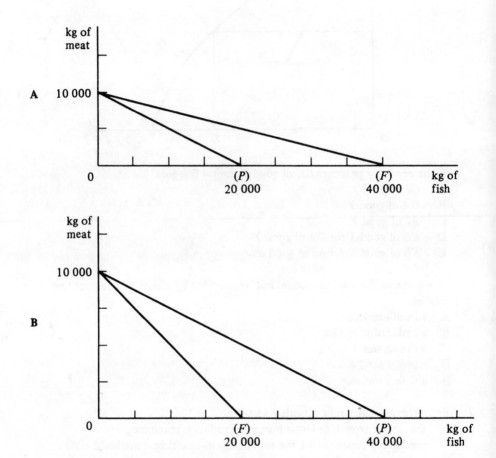

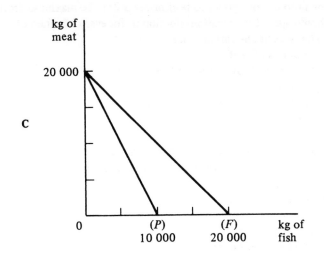

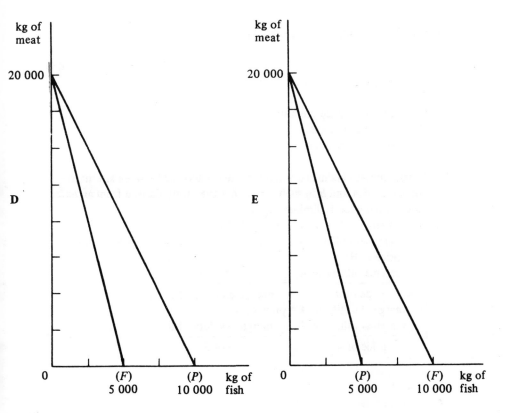

6 EXERCISES

9   Suppose the ratio of pork prices to beef prices is 2 : 1. To maximise profits a farmer should specialise in beef production if, for every kilogram of pork production he gives up, he can produce
  A   only $\frac{1}{2}$ kg or less of beef.
  B   more than $\frac{1}{2}$ kg but not as much as 1 kg of beef.
  C   exactly 1 kg of beef but no more.
  D   more than 1 kg but not as much as 2 kg of beef.
  E   more than 2 kg of beef.

10   Which one of the following facilities made available by a railway company acknowledges a divergence between private and social costs?
  A   restaurant cars
  B   cheap day return tickets
  C   waiting rooms
  D   sleeping compartments
  E   non-smoking compartments

Exercise 2   Theory of demand (1)

1   A fall in demand for petrol by private motorists is likely to follow a fall in
  A   the price of second-hand cars.
  B   the price of steel.
  C   motor insurance premiums.
  D   bus and train fares.
  E   motor-vehicle licence duty.

2   Satisfaction is maximised when income is allocated between alternative purchases of A and B in such a way that the utility derived from an extra unit of each good is diminishing and
  A   marginal utility of A = marginal utility of B
  B   (marginal utility of A) × (price of A) = (marginal utility of B) × (price of B)
  C $\dfrac{\text{marginal utility of } A}{\text{price of } A} = \dfrac{\text{price of } B}{\text{marginal utility of } B}$
  D   marginal utility of A = price of A
  E $\dfrac{\text{marginal utility of } A}{\text{price of } A} = \dfrac{\text{marginal utility of } B}{\text{price of } B}$

3

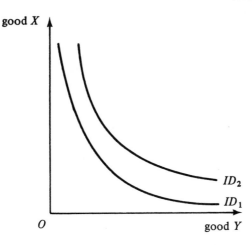

Which one of the following changes could cause an individual with a given money income to move from indifference curve ID_2 to ID_1?
A   a reduction in the prices of both good X and good Y
B   a reduction in the price of good X only
C   an increase in the price of good X only
D   an increase in the consumer's level of income
E   a reduction in the value-added tax on both goods

8 EXERCISES

4

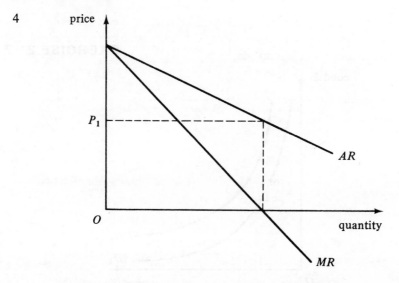

Given the straight-line average and marginal revenue curves in the above diagram, what is the value of the price elasticity of demand when price is below P_1?

A zero
B less than one but greater than zero
C one
D greater than one but less than infinity
E infinity

5

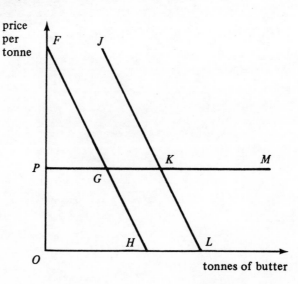

If a policy of price support for agriculture is introduced, the guaranteed minimum price per tonne of butter being *OP* and the price being maintained by intervention buying for stockpile, what will be the new effective demand curve, given that the original was *FGH*?

A   *JKL*
B   *JKM*
C   *FGM*
D   *PKM*
E   *PKL*

6   If the elasticity of demand for a commodity is equal to unity, the effect of a 1% fall in its price would be to
A   reduce revenue by 1%.
B   reduce revenue by 0.1%.
C   increase revenue by 0.1%.
D   increase revenue by 1%.
E   leave revenue unchanged.

7   The cross elasticity of demand of good X with respect to good Y is

A $\dfrac{\text{percentage change in quantity demanded of good } X}{\text{percentage change in price of good } Y}$

B $\dfrac{\text{percentage change in quantity demanded of good } Y}{\text{percentage change in price of good } X}$

C $\dfrac{\text{percentage change in quantity demanded of goods } X \text{ and } Y \text{ combined}}{\text{percentage change in their joint prices}}$

D $\dfrac{\text{percentage change in quantity demanded of good } X \text{ \textit{minus}} \text{ percentage change in quantity demanded of good } Y}{\text{percentage change in price of good } X \text{ \textit{minus}} \text{ percentage change in price of good } Y}$

E $\dfrac{\text{percentage change in quantity demanded of good } X}{\text{percentage change in quantity demanded of good } Y}$

8

average weekly household earnings	quantity of meat demanded per week
$40.00	8000 kg
$41.00	8600 kg

The income elasticity of demand for meat is

A   −0.33
B   +0.30
C   +0.53
D   +3.00
E   +5.35

9   In the diagram below, *PQ* is a consumption-possibility line for a consumer whose entire money income is spent on apples and oranges.

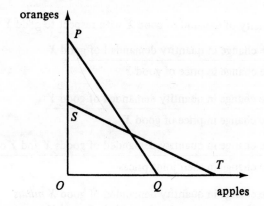

ST could represent the new consumption-possibility line following

A   a rise in his money income and a fall in both prices.
B   a rise in his money income, a fall in the price of oranges and a rise in the price of apples.
C   equal percentage falls in his money income and both prices.
D   a fall in his income and a fall in the price of apples.
E   a rise in the price of apples and a fall in the price of oranges.

10   *DD* in the diagram below represents the demand schedule for municipal bus services. At an initial fare *OF*, the number of journeys per day is *ON*.

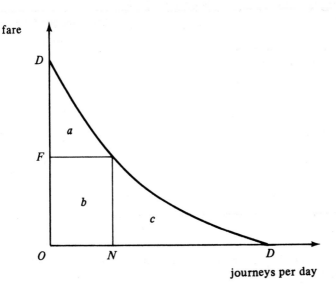

If the municipal bus authority now abolishes fares and provides free bus services, there will be an increase in consumers' surplus equal to

A   *b + c*.
B   *c − a*.
C   *c − b*.
D   *a + b*.
E   *c + b − a*.

Exercise 3   Theory of demand (2)

1   The demand curve for a product will shift to the right if
    A   the price of the product falls.
    B   a new source of the product is found.
    C   the prices of substitute products increase.
    D   there is an increase in the subsidy paid to producers of the product.
    E   there is a successful advertising campaign for a substitute product.

12 EXERCISES

Questions 2 and 3 refer to the following table which shows the demand schedule for a commodity.

price (£)	quantity demanded per year (tonnes)
10	0
9	2
8	3
7	4
6	5
5	6
4	7
3	7
2	9
1	10

2   The price elasticity of demand for an increase in price from £8 to £9, calculated from the table, is

A   0.375
B   0.625
C   1.0
D   2.66
E   3.0

3   In the table the price elasticity of demand is zero when the price

A   rises from £1 to £2.
B   rises from £3 to £4.
C   rises from £4 to £5.
D   falls from £7 to £6.
E   falls from £10 to £9.

4

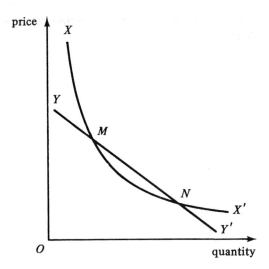

price

In the above diagram, the demand curve XX' is a rectangular hyperbola; the demand curve YY' is a straight line. If follows that

A XX' has the same elasticity at all points.

B YY' has the same elasticity at all points.

C YY' is less elastic than the curve XX' at the point M.

D YY' is more elastic at the point N than it is at the point M.

E XX' is more elastic at the point N than it is at the point M.

5   The direction of the income effect is such that it

A   may be positive, negative or zero.

B   is always negative.

C   may be positive or zero but is never negative.

D   may be negative or zero but is never positive.

E   is always positive.

14 EXERCISES

6   In the following diagram, *OABCDE* shows how a consumer's purchase of *X* varies with his income.

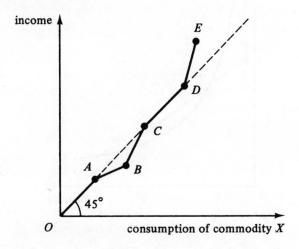

Within which of *OABCDE* is the income elasticity of demand for *X* greater than 0 and less than +1?

A   *AB* only
B   *OA* and *CD*
C   *AB* and *BC*
D   *BC* and *DE*
E   *DE* only

7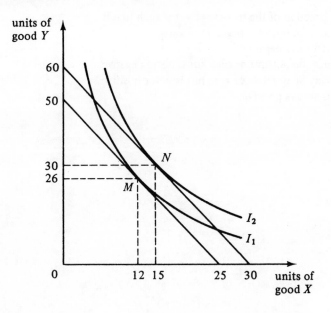

In the indifference map shown, the income elasticity of demand for good X for
the move from point M to point N lies within the range

  A   0.76 – 0.85
  B   0.86 – 0.95
  C   0.96 – 1.05
  D   1.06 – 1.15
  E   1.16 – 1.25

8   The diagram below shows the indifference map for consumer Jones with
respect to two goods A and B.

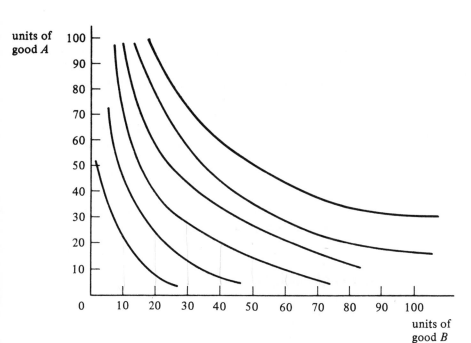

Jones has an income of £100 per week. The price of A is £1 per unit and
the price of B is £2 per unit. How many units of good B must he purchase per
week in order to maximise his welfare?

  A   10
  B   20
  C   30
  D   40
  E   50

9   The table below provides information on combinations of food and drink that give equal satisfaction to an individual.

amount of food (kilograms)	60	36	26	20	16	14
amount of drink (litres)		10	20	30	40	50	60

The individual's behaviour is

A   rational, because there is a diminishing rate of substitution of food for drink.

B   rational, because there is a constant rate of substitution of food for drink.

C   irrational, because there is a diminishing rate of substitution of food for drink.

D   irrational, because there is an increasing rate of substitution of food for drink.

E   irrational, because there is a constant rate of substitution of food for drink.

10   A consumer experiences a fall in his income while the prices of the two goods (A and B) he buys remain constant. If he buys the same quantity of A as before

A   the price elasticity of demand for A is higher than that for B.

B   the income elasticity of demand for good A is unity.

C   the income elasticity of demand for A is lower than that for B.

D   good A is a luxury and good B a necessity.

E   the cross elasticity of demand for B with respect to A is less than unity.

Exercise 4   Theory of supply (1)

1

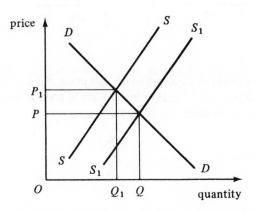

Which one of the following could explain the shift of the supply curve for a commodity from SS to $S_1 S_1$, as in the diagram above?

A a fall in price from OP_1 to OP
B an increase in quantity demanded from OQ_1 to OQ
C the imposition of a tax on the commodity
D improved production techniques in the industry producing the commodity
E an increase in the cost of the factors used in the production of the commodity

2 The supply curve of a commodity is such that at a price of 50 cents the quantity supplied is 1000 units and over the whole range of prices a price reduction of 1 cent results in a contraction in the quantity supplied of 20 units. It follows that
A supply is perfectly elastic.
B supply is of unitary elasticity.
C supply is inelastic over the whole range of prices.
D supply is elastic over the whole range of prices.
E as price increases the elasticity of supply increases.

3 An employer who pays a uniform wage to all his employees is considering hiring an extra employee. At present he hires 50 workers at £2.00 per worker per day. He has to raise the wage by 20p per day to attract an extra worker. The marginal cost of labour per day in this case is
A 20p
B £20.00
C £20.20
D £12.20
E £30.20

4 If marginal cost is increasing
A average cost must also be increasing.
B average cost must be greater than marginal cost.
C marginal cost must be equal to average cost.
D marginal cost must be greater than average cost.
E none of the above is necessarily true.

5 The following table relates the total output and the total costs of a firm.

output (units)	costs (£)
100	125
200	200
300	250
400	275
500	290

The firm's production function shows

A   increasing returns throughout.
B   decreasing returns thoughout.
C   increasing returns for output between 100 and 300 units and decreasing returns for output larger than 300 units.
D   decreasing returns for output between 100 and 300 units and increasing returns for output larger than 300 units.
E   constant returns throughout.

6 Where the slope of the total product curve is zero

A   average product is zero.
B   marginal product is zero.
C   marginal product is negative.
D   marginal product equals average product.
E   marginal product is greater than average product.

7 The table shows, for various levels of labour input, total output in physical units.

units of labour	1	2	3	4	5	6	7	8
total output	3	7	12	16	19	21	22	22

At which output level does the marginal physical product of labour equal the average product of labour?

A   22
B   19
C   16
D   12
E   7

8   Each curve in the diagram below describes the different combinations of capital and labour capable of producing the level of output indicated.

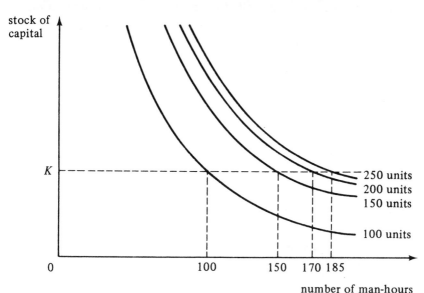

It may be deduced from the diagram that, with a fixed stock of capital, K, as output increases

A   the average product of capital diminishes.
B   short-run average costs fall faster than long-run average costs.
C   there are diseconomies of scale.
D   the marginal product of labour is constant.
E   the marginal product of labour increases.

9   Horizontal integration in an industry means amalgamation between firms
A   making different types of consumer goods.
B   at the secondary stage of production.
C   at different stages of production of the same end product.
D   marketing their products in the same geographical area.
E   at the same stage of production of the same end product.

10   External economies of scale in production may arise from
A   increased advertising.
B   reduction in the price of imports.
C   geographical concentration of firms.
D   growth in consumer income.
E   more efficient top management.

Exercise 5 Theory of supply (2)

1 The total supply of a commodity to a market is provided by three firms, 1, 2 and 3, whose supply curves are represented respectively by S_1S_1', S_2S_2', and S_3S_3', while S_1TT' represents the aggregate supply curve.

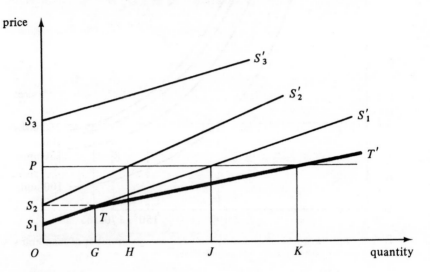

If the market price is fixed at OP, what will be the composition of aggregate supply?

	firm 1	firm 2	firm 3
A	OG	HJ	GH
B	OG	GH	HK
C	OH	zero	HK
D	OJ	JK	zero
E	zero	OJ	JK

2 The short-run supply curve of a firm under perfect competition is obtained from the rising portion of which one of the following cost schedules?
A marginal cost
B total cost
C average fixed cost
D average variable cost
E average total cost

3 If the supply of a good is perfectly elastic with respect to price, a tax on
each unit of the good will
A reduce the amount which the producer receives for one unit by the
amount of the tax.
B raise the price of one unit to consumers by the amount of the tax.
C raise the price of one unit to consumers by an amount greater than the
tax.
D raise the price of one unit to consumers by an amount dependent on
the price elasticity of demand.
E leave the price of one unit to consumers unchanged.

4 If production is being carried on under conditions of diminishing physical
returns to a factor
A adding more of the variable input must result in a reduction in total
output.
B total output can only be increased by adding to the fixed input.
C the cost of hiring additional units of the variable input becomes steadily
greater.
D increasing amounts of the variable input are needed to obtain each
successive unit of additional output.
E a proportionate increase in each of the factor inputs produces a less
than proportionate increase in output.

5 In perfect competition an entrepreneur achieves the least-cost combination
of inputs X and Y when

A $\dfrac{MPP(X)}{P(Y)} = \dfrac{MPP(Y)}{P(X)}$

B $\dfrac{MRP(X)}{P(Y)} = \dfrac{MRP(Y)}{P(X)}$

C $\dfrac{MPP(X)}{P(X)} = \dfrac{MPP(Y)}{P(Y)}$

D $\dfrac{ARP(X)}{P(X)} = \dfrac{ARP(Y)}{P(Y)}$

E $\dfrac{MRP(X)}{ARP(X)} = \dfrac{MRP(Y)}{ARP(Y)}$

($MRP(X)$ is the marginal revenue product of X, $P(X)$ the price of X, $MPP(X)$
the marginal physical product of X and $ARP(X)$ the average revenue product
of X. Similarly for Y.)

6 The long-run average cost curve shows the
  A average unit cost of variable factor inputs.
  B average unit cost of fixed factor inputs.
  C unit cost of replacing the stock of fixed assets.
  D minimum unit cost of every feasible level of output.
  E minimum amount by which cost is increased when output is expanded.

7 If the average variable costs of a firm are falling as output increases then
  A average fixed costs are constant.
  B total costs are constant.
  C average total costs are falling.
  D marginal costs are greater than average costs of production.
  E marginal costs are constant for the entire range of output.

8 Which one of the following curves correctly depicts the average cost of operating an under-utilised bus service between Glasgow and Edinburgh?

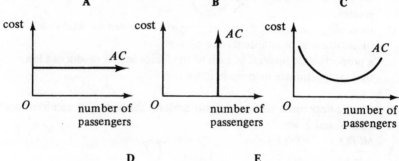

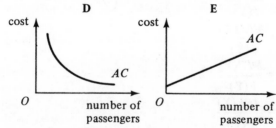

9 If a payroll tax is to effect a reduction of the proportion of labour to capital in industry, which one of the following conditions must hold?
  A Firms are producing under diminishing returns.
  B Firms are faced with inelastic demands for their products.
  C The work force is largely composed of young people.
  D Labour and capital are substitutes in production.
  E The average rate of return on capital is diminishing.

10   In order to cut down fuel consumption by motor cars, a government
      introduces a new sales tax on cars over 2000 cc. As a result, producers of
      cars in this category find that on each car sold their net revenue after tax
      falls by the amount of the tax. For these cars the price elasticity of
      A   supply is unity.
      B   supply is infinite.
      C   demand is zero.
      D   demand is unity.
      E   demand is infinite.

Exercise 6   Price and output (1)

1   Which one of the following is **not** consistent with perfect competition?
      A   large numbers of producers and consumers
      B   advertising by individual firms
      C   one market price
      D   a homogeneous product
      E   a perfectly elastic demand curve for each firm

2   The demand curve for product X slopes downwards from left to right. If
      product X has to compete with many other similar products and if entry
      into this particular market is free, the firm producing X
      A   must act like a price-taker and therefore equate price with marginal
           cost.
      B   enjoys monopoly power and therefore can earn supernormal profits
           in the long run.
      C   will in the long run operate at minimum average total cost like a
           firm in perfect competition.
      D   will in the long run make only normal profit since short-run profits
           will be eroded by the activities of new entrants to the industry.
      E   will sell less at all prices as more firms enter the industry and its
           demand curve becomes steeper.

3　The diagram below shows the cost and revenue curves of a firm which is producing *ON* units of output.

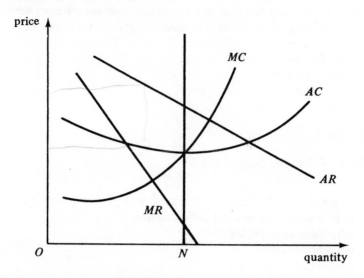

To maximise profits the firm should

A　increase output until $AC = AR$.
B　increase output until $MC = AR$.
C　reduce output until $MC = MR$.
D　reduce output until $MR = AC$.
E　continue to produce at *ON*.

4　Which one of the following is **not** a characteristic of the perfectly competitive firm when the industry is in equilibrium?

A　Profits are maximised when marginal costs are equal to marginal revenue.
B　Price is equal to marginal cost.
C　Output is produced at minimum average cost.
D　Output is produced at minimum marginal cost.
E　For an output less than the optimum, marginal cost is below average cost.

5　The diagram opposite represents the total cost and total revenue curves of a firm operating under perfectly competitive conditions.

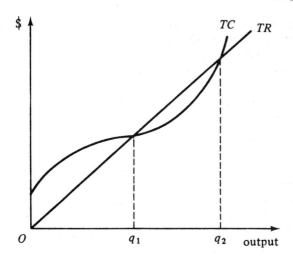

The firm maximises profits
A   at output levels below q_1.
B   at output level q_1.
C   between output levels q_1 and q_2.
D   at output level q_2.
E   at output levels above q_2.

6   Although supernormal profits can be made by a firm operating under
conditions of perfect competition or imperfect competition, only in the
former case will
A $MR = AR$.
B $MR = MC$.
C $AR = AC$.
D $MC = AC$.
E $AR > AC$.

7   A stationer sells birthday cards at 10p each but gives a special offer for all
purchases over 10 cards by reducing the price to 9p per card for the whole
purchase. If a customer, who would otherwise have bought 10 cards, now
buys 11, then the marginal revenue to the stationer from this sale is
A   equal to the price.
B   greater than average revenue.
C   positive but less than average revenue.
D   negative.
E   the same as the marginal revenue for the tenth card.

8   If the demand and supply of a product in a competitive market are both permanently increased by 10% at each and every price, the new long-run market equilibrium occurs at a

    A   5% increase in both price and sales.
    B   10% higher price with unchanged sales.
    C   10% higher sales level with unchanged price.
    D   10% higher sales level with a 10% lower price.
    E   10% lower sales level with a 10% higher price.

9   In an oligopolistic market a firm will be wary of reducing its prices on its own because

    A   other firms may decide to leave their prices unchanged.
    B   this may lead to price reductions on the part of its competitors.
    C   this may lead to the entry of new firms into the industry.
    D   its demand curve is perfectly inelastic.
    E   firms in such a market always agree with one another on prices.

10   The diagram below illustrates the demand for and supply of coal mined in a country.

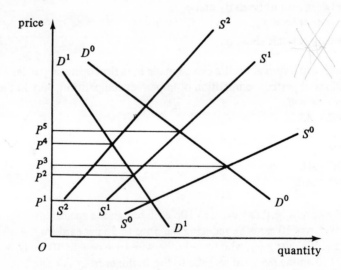

    Which one of the following would best explain an increase in the price of coal from OP^3 to OP^5?

    A   an increase in labour costs
    B   a subsidy for the coal industry
    C   an increase in the industrial demand for coal
    D   a fall in the price of oil
    E   an increase in the duty on imported pertroleum

Exercise 7   Price and output (2)

1   The diagram below shows the demand for and supply of butter.

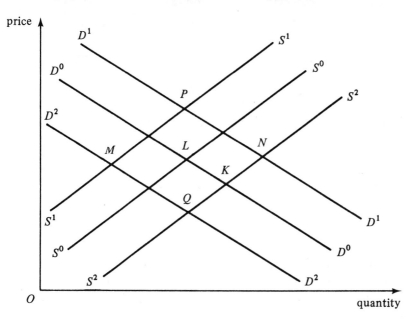

The market is initially in equilibrium at point L. The government then grants a subsidy to butter producers while at the same time the price of margarine falls considerably. The new market equilibrium will be at point

A K.
B M.
C N.
D P.
E Q.

2   If the current output of a perfectly competitive firm is at a level at which marginal cost is less than marginal revenue, profit maximisation would imply

A   increased output and a higher price.
B   decreased output and a higher price.
C   increased output and a lower price.
D   decreased output and an unchanged price.
E   increased output and an unchanged price.

3   The following table gives a firm's costs for various levels of output.

units of output	average fixed cost ($)	average variable cost ($)	average total cost ($)
2	5.00	8.00	13.00
3	3.33	6.00	9.33
4	2.50	5.00	7.50
5	2.00	6.00	8.00
6	1.66	8.00	9.66

What will the output of the firm be in the short run if it can sell its output at a unit price of $5?

A   2 units
B   3 units
C   4 units
D   5 units
E   6 units

4   The curves S and D are respectively the market supply and demand curves of a competitive industry. The curves MC and MR are respectively the marginal cost and marginal revenue curves of a monopolist who takes over the industry.

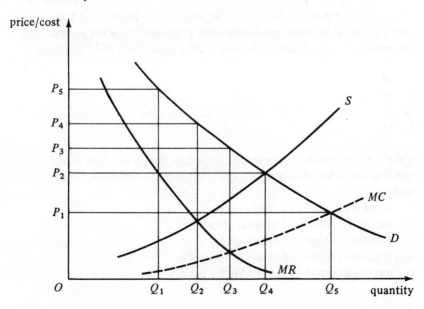

In the circumstances shown in the diagram, the profit-maximising monopolist would produce

A OQ_1
B OQ_2
C OQ_3
D OQ_4
E OQ_5

5   The diagram below illustrates a firm operating under conditions of imperfect
    competition.

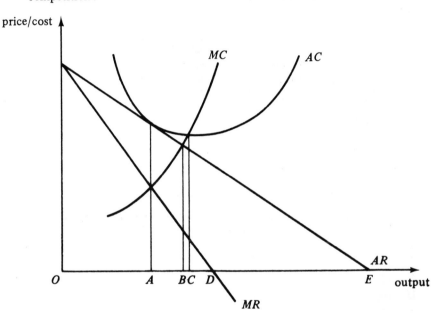

What is its equilibrium level of output?
A OA
B OB
C OC
D OD
E OE

6   Suppose it became possible as a result of a technical innovation to build
    houses with one-half of the labour at present required. Which of the follow-
    ing is the **least** likely to increase as a direct consequence?
    A   the price of land
    B   the price of building materials
    C   the price of existing houses
    D   the income of estate agents
    E   the profits of building firms

7   If, after being free of tax, the profit of a profit-maximising monopolist is taxed at a rate of 25%, he will

     A   raise price and reduce output.
     B   raise price and maintain output.
     C   maintain price and increase output.
     D   reduce price and raise output.
     E   leave price and output unchanged.

8   The table below shows demand and supply schedules for grapes in a certain area and over a given period of time. The equilibrium price is 15p per kg.

price per kg	amount demand (thousand kg)	amount supplied (thousand kg)
30p	1	12
25p	2	9
20p	3	7
15p	5	5
10p	7	3
5p	10	1

If the government introduced a tax of 10p per kg, what would be the new equilibrium price charged to consumers?

     A   25p
     B   20p
     C   15p
     D   10p
     E   5p

9   The diagram below shows the market supply and demand schedules for
    a particular agricultural product.

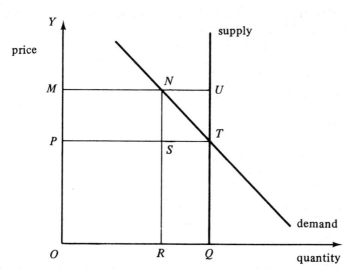

The government decides to fix the price at *OM* by buying in the open
market. Which area in the diagram represents the government's expenditure?

A   *OMNR*
B   *RNUQ*
C   *PMNT*
D   *RNTQ*
E   *NUTS*

10 The information in the table below relates to the current operations of a
    firm which has three plants and sells its product at £10 per unit in a perfect
    market. Each plant has a U-shaped average cost curve.

plant	X	Y	Z
average total cost	£11	£9	£9
marginal cost	£11	£8	£11

In order to maximise profits, the firm in the long run will

A   shut down *X*, expand production at *Y* and reduce production at *Z*.
B   shut down *X*, reduce production at *Y* and expand production at *Z*.
C   expand production at *X*, shut down *Y* and reduce production at *Z*.
D   expand production at *X*, reduce production at *Y* and shut down *Z*.
E   reduce production at *X*, expand production at *Y* and shut down *Z*.

Exercise 8 Theory of distribution

1 A profit-maximising firm in a perfectly competitive industry, which buys labour in a perfectly competitive market, will **not** employ labour beyond the point where the value of its marginal product is
   A equal to the value of the marginal product of capital.
   B equal to the unit price of output.
   C at a maximum.
   D equal to its price.
   E zero.

2 Rent is a payment to a factor of production
   A in excess of its transfer earnings.
   B equal to the value of its expected earnings.
   C equal to its marginal revenue product.
   D equal to the value of its marginal product.
   E equal to its supply price.

3 The graph below shows the indifference map between leisure and money income for a worker employed by firm X. The line MN shows the range of opportunities open to the worker if the wage rate is £0.75 per hour.

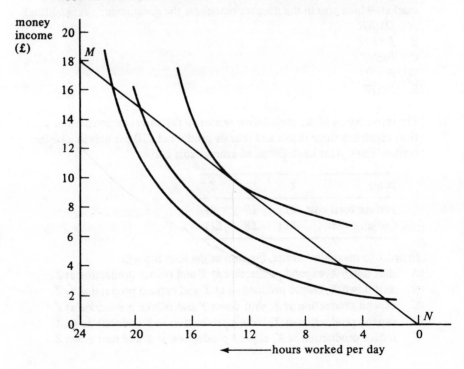

When the firm reduces its wage rate to £0.50 per hour the worker will
maximise his welfare by
A   working 8 hours per day.
B   working 12 hours per day.
C   working 14 hours per day.
D   earning an income of £1.80 per day.
E   earning an income of £10 per day.

4   If a trade union leader is trying to raise the wages of his members in a firm,
     he should **oppose** the introduction of
     A   capital-saving inventions within the firm.
     B   a payroll tax on the labour of the firm.
     C   an advertising campaign for the goods of the firm.
     D   a tariff on imports competitive with the goods of the firm.
     E   measures to extend the period of apprenticeship training.

5   Which one of the following could be expected to raise the rate of profit
     in an economy?
     A   a ban on the export of capital
     B   a general freeze on prices but not on incomes
     C   an appreciation of the exchange rate
     D   labour-saving technical progress
     E   the removal of all tariffs on imported consumer goods .

6   'Normal Profit' is defined as
     A   an average of profit levels over a number of years.
     B   the level of profit earned when all variable factors are paid their
          marginal revenue products.
     C   the level of profit which in the long run is just sufficient to keep
          a firm in the industry.
     D   the level of profit achieved by equating marginal cost and marginal
          revenue.
     E   any difference between total revenue and total cost.

7   If, as its contribution to International Women's Year, a government legis-
     lates for equal pay for women, which one of the following would be likely
     to occur?
     A   a fall in the level of male employment
     B   a fall in the level of female employment
     C   a fall in total industry costs
     D   a fall in the marginal revenue product schedule for men
     E   a rise in the sales of products intensive in the use of female labour

8   A law greatly increasing the payments which employers must pay to
    employees in the event of redundancy is likely to
    A   reduce the number of people entering the labour force.
    B   increase the rate of voluntary resignations.
    C   lead to the substitution of labour for capital.
    D   reduce wage rates to finance the redundancy payments.
    E   encourage overtime working rather than the employment of additional
        labour.

9   The elasticity of demand for labour in an industry will be greater
    A   the greater the difficulty of substituting capital for labour.
    B   the greater the elasticity of demand for the finished product.
    C   the lower its marginal revenue productivity.
    D   the shorter the period of training required in the industry.
    E   the lower the level of unemployment in the economy.

10 In the diagram below, the line SS illustrates the long-run supply of labour
    to a particular occupation.

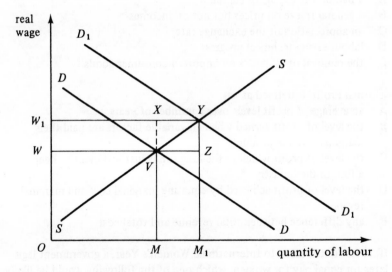

An increase in demand from DD to D_1D_1 will result in an increase in the
economic rent accruing to the labour force represented by the area
A WW_1XV.
B WW_1YV.
C MM_1YV.
D YXV.
E WW_1YZ.

Exercise 9   National Income accounting

1   At the time of his retirement from full-time employment, Mr X was earning
£4000 per annum. He and his wife received a state pension of £500 per
annum and he also received an occupational pension of £1000 per annum.
He undertook part-time work earning £250 per annum and this did not
affect his pension rights. The effect of all this on the National Income in
a full year would be to reduce it by
A   £4000
B   £3750
C   £3250
D   £2500
E   £2250

2   In an economy in which there is neither foreign trade nor household
savings, government expenditure is equal to net tax receipts from households. The following data are in £ million.

Gross National Product	200
Private consumption	160
Public consumption	10

Investment by firms is
A   £10 million.
B   £20 million.
C   £30 million.
D   £40 million.
E   £50 million.

3 Consider the following data:

	£m
Consumers' expenditure	29000
Public authorities' current expenditure on goods and services	8000
Gross domestic fixed capital formation	8000
Subsidies	1000
Imports and property income paid abroad	11000
Taxes on expenditure	8000
Exports and property income from abroad	12000
Capital consumption	4000

What is the country's Gross National Product at market prices?
A £35000 m
B £36000 m
C £39000 m
D £40000 m
E £46000 m

4 Gross National Product at market prices exceeds Net National Product at factor cost by
A Capital Consumption + Expenditure Taxes − Subsidies.
B Net Income from abroad + Capital Consumption.
C Transfer Payments + Expenditure Taxes − Subsidies.
D Net Income from abroad + Expenditure Taxes − Subsidies.
E Capital Consumption.

5 Which one of the following is included in Net National Income at factor cost calculated by the 'Income Method'?
A the trading surplus of the Post Office
B the prizes received by the winners of a national lottery run by the government
C an owner's proceeds from the sale of his house
D capital consumption
E the interest received by holders of government bonds

6 To compute a firm's contribution to Gross National Product on a value-added basis, we must deduct from the value at market prices of the goods it has produced
A all purchases from other business firms.
B any undistributed profits.
C depreciation.
D all sales to other business firms.
E all indirect taxes paid.

7   Which one of the following items is **not** treated as a transfer payment in National Income accounting?
   A   famine relief payments
   B   interest on the National Debt paid to residents
   C   unemployment benefit
   D   educational scholarships
   E   police force pay

8   Changes in the standard of living of a country are best indicated by the growth in the
   A   total real National Income.
   B   total monetary National Income.
   C   real income per member of the working population.
   D   monetary income per member of the population.
   E   real income per member of the population.

9   What should be substituted for x in the following equation?

   Gross National Product $- x =$ Consumption + Net Investment
   A   depreciation
   B   subsidies
   C   exports
   D   undistributed corporate profits
   E   residual error

10   In the calculation of the U.K.'s Gross National Product, the value of the nationalised steel industry's output used by the car industry is **not** included because
   A   the steel industry is publicly owned.
   B   the raw materials for steel production are imported.
   C   the raw materials for steel production have been included.
   D   most of the steel is taken out of stocks which have already been counted in previous periods.
   E   the value of the steel is included in the value of the cars produced.

38 EXERCISES

Exercise 10   Theory of income determination (1)

1   In a simple Keynesian system with a constant level of investment the
     equality between savings and investment is achieved by changes in the
     A   volume of investment.
     B   price of investment goods.
     C   price of consumer goods.
     D   rate of interest.
     E   level of National Income.

2   The following data represent a consumption function for an economy.

income (£m)	consumption (£m)
120	116
140	132
160	148
180	164
200	180
220	196

     What is the value of the marginal propensity to consume in this economy?
     A   0.00
     B   0.80
     C   0.90
     D   0.91
     E   0.98

3   In a full employment economy, where the marginal propensity to consume
     of pensioners exceeds that of taxpayers, government expenditure on pensions
     is increased by $x million. In order to avoid an inflationary gap, taxation
     must be
     A   increased by less than $x million.
     B   increased by $x million.
     C   increased by more than $x million.
     D   reduced by $x million.
     E   reduced by more than $x million.

4   An open economy with no government sector is represented in the diagram below.

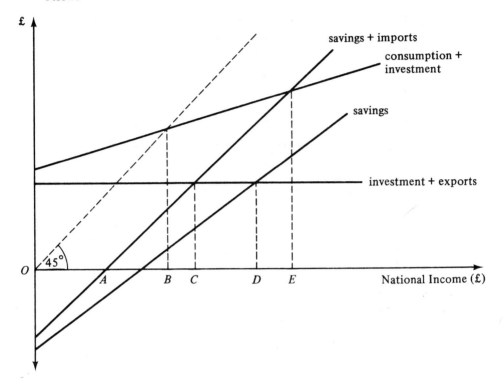

What is the equilibrium level of National Income?
A   *OA*
B   *OB*
C   *OC*
D   *OD*
E   *OE*

5   In a fully employed economy, other things being equal, which one of the following would by itself be inflationary?
A   an increase in the rate of income tax on higher incomes
B   an increase in the demand for exports
C   an increase in the productivity of labour
D   an increase in the real Gross National Product
E   an increase in personal saving

For Questions 6 and 7 use the information given in the diagram below.

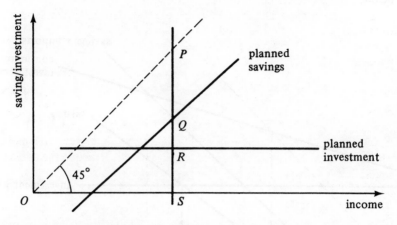

6   Which distance represents unplanned increase in stocks?
     A   *PQ*
     B   *PR*
     C   *PS*
     D   *QR*
     E   *RS*

7   Which distance indicates consumption expenditure?
     A   *PQ*
     B   *PR*
     C   *PS*
     D   *QR*
     E   *QS*

8   In a closed economy with no government sector, given that National Income
     in year 1 is 1000, and that the marginal propensity to save is 0.2, what is
     the National Income in year 2 if there is an additional investment of 100,
     assuming no time lags?
     A   500
     B   1125
     C   1225
     D   1500
     E   5100

9   Let C = Consumption, I = Investment, X = Exports, M = Imports, Y = National
    Income, and b = marginal propensity to consume.
        If $C = 10 + bY$, $I = 5$, $X = 12$, $M = 16$ and $b = \frac{3}{4}$, the equilibrium level of Y
    will be
    A   172
    B   108
    C   44
    D   36
    E   27

10 If, when the National Income is in equilibrium, there is a decrease in imports,
    which one of the following changes of equal value would restore the initial
    equilibrium?
    A   a decrease in savings
    B   an increase in government spending
    C   a decrease in investment
    D   an increase in exports
    E   a decrease in taxation

Exercise 11   Theory of income determination (2)

1   It has been observed that in a closed economy an autonomous increase in
    net investment eventually caused (a) an increase in real income equal to
    three times the increase in net investment, (b) an increase in employment,
    (c) no change in real income per employee. It may be reasonably deduced
    from these facts that
    A   the liquidity trap prevented the multiplier from working.
    B   two-thirds of marginal income was consumed.
    C   net investment was confined to the manufacturing sector of the economy.
    D   the marginal propensity to save had increased by one-third.
    E   the autonomous increase was not maintained indefinitely.

2   Which one of the following would cause the marginal efficiency of capital
    to fall?
    A   a rise in rates of interest
    B   a reduction in the marginal propensity to save
    C   a reduction in estimated future profits
    D   a reduction in liquidity preference
    E   an increase in depreciation allowances against taxation

3   An analysis of expenditure by households at different income levels suggests
     that average propensity to consume (*APC*) is equal to the marginal propen-
     sity to consume (*MPC*) over low income levels. However, at high income
     levels, *MPC* declines with income and is less than the *APC*. Which one of the
     following describes these findings?

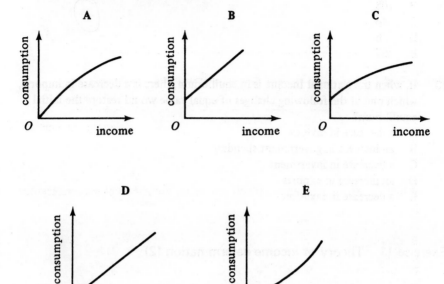

4   Given unemployed resources, £100 million of additional government expend
     ture on goods and services has a greater impact on National Income than
     does £100 million of tax remission because
     A   some of the tax remission will be saved.
     B   the multiplier applies only to investment expenditure.
     C   only government expenditure implies deficit financing.
     D   government expenditure is additional to private expenditure.
     E   taxes have no effect on disposable income.

5   In the diagram below, S is the savings function and I_1 and I_2 are different
    levels of investment.

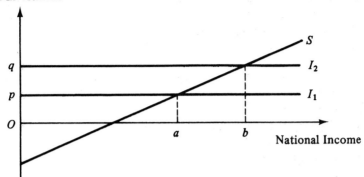

total savings
and investment

If investment increases from I_1 to I_2 the value of the multiplier is represented
by

A Ob/pq.
B Oq/Op.
C ab/pq.
D ab/Op.
E pq/ab.

6   In 1978 a closed economy with a fixed labour force and no government
    sector is in full employment equilibrium with investment equal to $1000 m
    and consumption $29000 m. The marginal propensity to consume is 0.8
    and the investment in 1978 is sufficient to increase labour productivity
    by 3%. How much additional investment is needed in 1979 if the economy
    is to stay at full employment equilibrium?

A $174 m
B $180 m
C $720 m
D $870 m
E $900 m

7 Government attempts to increase employment by increasing government spending will be rendered less effective if at the same time there is an increase in the
   A value of the multiplier.
   B marginal propensity to consume.
   C marginal rate of taxation.
   D level of private investment.
   E sales of exports.

8 If gross investment falls to zero, what prevents National Income from falling to zero?
   A consumption
   B the Bank Rate (minimum lending rate)
   C the multiplier
   D the accelerator
   E imports

9 The marginal propensity to import is defined as
   A the total volume of imports divided by the National Income.
   B the National Income divided by the total volume of imports.
   C the induced change in the volume of imports divided by the change in the National Income.
   D the proportionate change in the volume of imports divided by the proportionate change in import prices.
   E the proportionate change in the volume of imports divided by the proportionate change in the National Income.

10 The effect on National Income of a rise in the marginal propensity to import would be to
   A increase it.
   B lower it.
   C leave it unchanged and redistribute income in favour of the poor.
   D leave it unchanged and redistribute income in favour of the rich.
   E leave it unchanged but worsen the balance of trade.

Exercise 12   Money and prices (1)

1   Which one of the following is **not** a function of money?
  A   unit of account
  B   source of credit
  C   store of value
  D   medium of exchange
  E   standard for deferred payments

2   The Retail Price Index is 'weighted' in order to take account of
  A   seasonal fluctuations in prices.
  B   movements in wholesale prices.
  C   the tendency of the general price level to rise.
  D   the change of base year which is made from time to time.
  E   the relative importance of various items in the general pattern of consumption.

3   The expenditure patterns of three consumers are given in the table below, together with price indices for each item for year 1 and year 2.

commodity	percentage of total expenditure of Robinson	Smith	Jones	index of prices in year 1	index of prices in year 2
food	40	40	20	100	100
housing	50	30	30	100	150
durables	10	30	50	100	50

If their money incomes and preferences have stayed the same over this period, for whom has real income fallen?
  A   Robinson only
  B   Smith only
  C   Jones only
  D   Robinson and Smith
  E   Jones and Smith

4   A central bank engages in expansionist open-market operations when it
  A   sells securities to non-government buyers.
  B   buys securities from non-government holders.
  C   uses moral suasion on institutions in the money market.
  D   reduces its minimum lending rate.
  E   reduces compulsory deposits at the central bank.

5   Which one of the following is a liability of a U.K. commercial bank?
     A   loans to discount houses
     B   money at call
     C   deposit accounts of customers
     D   special deposits at the Bank of England
     E   overdrafts incurred by small traders

6   If all banks observe a 20% reserve asset ratio, by how much can the banking system increase deposits in response to a new deposit of $100?
     A $100
     B $200
     C $400
     D $500
     E $2000

7   If an Accepting House discounts a Bill of Exchange valued at £1000 in 3 months' time for £980, the discount rate per annum is
     A   4%
     B   8%
     C   9.8%
     D   12%
     E   20%

8   The crude Quantity Theory of Money states that
     A $M = PV/T$.
     B   prices vary proportionately with the quantity of money in circulation.
     C   the velocity of circulation increases as the price level rises.
     D   the supply of money varies with the transactions demand for money.
     E $MP = VT$.

9   Which one of the following directly influences the speculative demand for money?
     A   the value of current transactions
     B   the marginal propensity to consume
     C   the marginal efficiency of capital
     D   the expected level of interest rates
     E   the income velocity of circulation of money

10   Which of the following measures is/are consistent with the objective of reducing demand inflation?

     (1) raising interest rates
     (2) lowering public expenditure
     (3) intensifying hire purchase controls

A   1, 2 and 3 are consistent.
B   1 and 2 only are consistent.
C   2 and 3 only are consistent.
D   Only 1 is consistent.
E   Only 3 is consistent.

Exercise 13   Money and prices (2)

1   A necessary condition for money to have value is that it is
   A   backed by gold.
   B   issued by the central bank.
   C   limited in supply.
   D   tied to the U.S. dollar.
   E   of intrinsic worth.

2   Comparisons of price indices over long periods of time are difficult because
   A   people's buying habits change.
   B   the quantity of goods demanded alters with price changes.
   C   the value of money may not remain constant.
   D   technological progress may mean that prices will fall.
   E   the amount of money spent may not remain constant.

3

	year 1	year 2
hourly wage rate	50 pence	60 pence
price index	120	110

The table shows that between years 1 and 2, using year 1 as the base, the hourly wage rate in real terms has
   A   fallen by 10%.
   B   remained constant.
   C   risen by 10%.
   D   risen by 20%.
   E   risen by more than 20%.

4   Which one of the following is **not** a tool of monetary policy?
   A   controlling government expenditure
   B   influencing rates of interest
   C   controlling the stock of money
   D   managing the National Debt
   E   controlling the availability of credit

5   A fall in the market price of fixed interest securities indicates that
   A   the market rate of interest has risen.
   B   the marginal productivity of capital has fallen.
   C   liquidity preference has decreased.
   D   the supply of money has increased.
   E   the income velocity of circulation of money has fallen.

6   If the Bank of England sells securities for £10 million on the open market, then the commercial banks
   A   need take no action because their assets and liabilities are both reduced by the same amount.
   B   must reduce their existing liquid assets.
   C   must reduce their advances by an amount dependent upon their existing liquid reserves.
   D   can increase advances by £10 million, provided there is a sufficient demand for credit.
   E   can increase advances by more than £10 million if their liquid assets exceed the required minimum.

7   In a closed economy producing a variety of goods, the average price per unit of finished output is \$20, the number of units of output of all types is 500 and the income velocity of circulation of money per annum is 4. The volume of money in circulation is
   A   \$100
   B   \$2000
   C   \$2500
   D   \$10 000
   E   \$40 000

8   If the central bank reduces the quantity of money, other things remaining constant, what will be the effect on interest rates and fixed interest security prices?

	interest rates	*fixed interest security prices*
A	fall	rise
B	fall	fall
C	fall	indeterminate
D	rise	fall
E	rise	indeterminate

9   The diagram below illustrates hypothetical equilibrium positions in the
bond market. L_1 and L_2 are liquidity preference curves. M_1, M_2 and M_3
represent different levels of money supply.

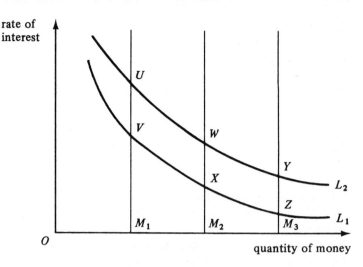

Other things being equal, which one of the following movements could
represent the effect of an increased demand for money?
A X to V
B X to W
C W to Y
D Y to Z
E Z to X

10   If a country has a deficit on its balance of payments the domestic money
supply is likely to
A   fall, because importers have to exchange domestic money to obtain
foreign currency.
B   remain unchanged, because the balance of payments always balances.
C   remain unchanged, because imports are bought with foreign currency.
D   rise, because the counterpart of the deficit will take the form of a
foreign loan.
E   rise, because domestic residents buy the extra goods which a deficit
implies.

50 EXERCISES

Exercise 14   International trade (1)

1   Which one of the following conditions **must** exist if international trade is to occur?
   A   no transport costs
   B   constant returns to scale in all industries
   C   equal opportunity cost ratios
   D   limited mobility of factors of production between countries
   E   limited mobility of factors of production within a country

2

	wheat (tonnes)	whisky (litres)
U.S.A.	30	20
U.K.	20	10

   If the above outputs represent one day's labour in each country
   A   the U.K. has an absolute advantage in the production of both commodities.
   B   the U.K. has a comparative advantage in producing wheat.
   C   the U.K. has a higher productivity of labour.
   D   trade is to neither country's advantage.
   E   trade will benefit only the U.S.A.

3   Which one of the following would be an item in the U.K. balance of payments on current account?
   A   the purchase of a controlling interest in British Rail by Americans
   B   the payment of dividends to foreigners owning shares in U.K. companies
   C   the 'recycling' of oil revenues earned by Arab states by the purchase of U.K. long-term bonds
   D   the purchase of a British wildlife park by foreign financiers
   E   the receipt of a loan by the U.K. government from the International Monetary Fund

4   If flexible exchange rates operate between the U.K. and the U.S.A., which one of the following, other things being equal, would bring about an appreciation in the exchange value of sterling?
   A   American companies buying factories in the U.K.
   B   American citizens buying Japanese rather than British cars
   C   U.K. citizens buying American company shares
   D   U.K. citizens spending more money in the U.S.A while on holiday
   E   foreign exchange speculators anticipating a rise in the exchange value of the U.S. dollar

5   The *terms of trade* are
    A   international trading agreements such as the General Agreement on
        Tariffs and Trade.
    B   the ratio of export prices to import prices.
    C   the rate at which one can exchange the domestic currency for foreign
        exchange.
    D   the ratio of exports to imports.
    E   the gap between invisible exports and imports.

6   The following information is given in the balance of payments accounts
    of a country.

	£m
Exports	2000
Imports	1650
Net military expenditure overseas	500
Profits from overseas subsidiaries of domestic companies	200
Net exports of banking and other services	575
Capital investment abroad	1500
Balancing item	20
Net monetary movements	855

    On current account this country is in
    A   deficit by £875m.
    B   deficit by £855m.
    C   surplus by £350m.
    D   surplus by £425m.
    E   surplus by £625m.

7   Devaluation of a country's currency is **not** likely to improve its balance
    of payments if
    A   it has unemployed resources.
    B   a significant proportion of its trade is invisible.
    C   the demand for exports is price elastic.
    D   the demand for imports is price elastic.
    E   the sum of the price elasticities of demand for exports and imports
        is less than one.

8 Suppose there are two countries in the world, X and Y. Two goods, corn and wool are produced. Relative opportunity costs are constant in each country. If X and Y specialise completely in the production of either corn or wool, the production possibilities are shown below.

	units of corn	units of wool
country X	300	200
country Y	400	100

Which one of the following rates of exchange between corn and wool could occur if X and Y traded freely?

A   6 units of corn for 1 unit of wool
B   2 units of corn for 1 unit of wool
C   1 unit of corn for 1 unit of wool
D   1 unit of corn for 2 units of wool
E   1 unit of corn for 6 units of wool

9 Following a depreciation in the exchange rate of the £ sterling, a British company keeps the American $ price of its exports unchanged. Other things being equal, the result will be

A   an increase in demand for the company's products in the U.S.A.
B   a reduction in the $ value of its U.S. sales.
C   a reduction in the £ value of its U.S. sales.
D   an increase in its profit margins on exports to the U.S.A.
E   a reduction in the relative price of the company's products in the U.S.A.

10 Given a fixed exchange rate, other things being equal, a country's reserves will be increased by

A   a reduction in merchandise exports.
B   a reduction in long-term investment abroad.
C   a reduction in short-term liabilities to foreigners.
D   an increase in imports of services.
E   an increase in transfer payments to foreigners.

Exercise 15   International trade (2)

1 A country's terms of trade worsen when

A   the total value of imports increases faster than the total value of exports.
B   the total value of visible and invisible credits on current account increases faster than the total value of visible and invisible debits.
C   trading partners devalue their currencies.
D   the volume of imports increases faster than the volume of exports.
E   the ratio of export prices to import prices falls.

2   Which one of the following is most likely to be a consequence of the devaluation of a country's currency, not accompanied by other measures?
   A   a reduction in domestic prices
   B   a reduction in the level of unemployment
   C   a reduction in money incomes
   D   a reduction in the rate of economic growth
   E   a loss of foreign currency reserves

3   Which one of the following does **not** provide an argument in favour of a policy of protection in international trade?
   A   It protects newly developed industries from foreign competition.
   B   It ensures the greatest gains from specialisation.
   C   It helps strategic but uncompetitive industries to survive.
   D   It prevents 'dumping'.
   E   It provides a weapon for bargaining in trade negotiations.

54 EXERCISES

Questions 4 and 5 relate to the diagram below which shows the demand and supply conditions for pounds sterling in international money markets. With demand and supply curves D^0D^0 and S^0S^0 the initial equilibrium exchange rate is 2 U.S. dollars to the pound sterling.

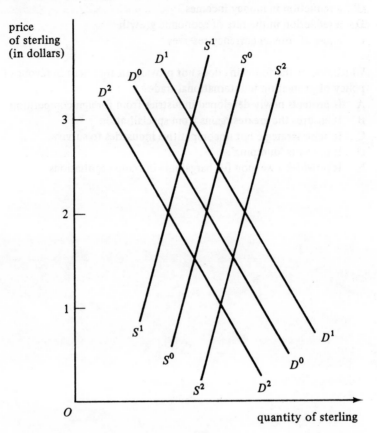

4   The demand curve D^0D^0 shifts to the right to D^1D^1 and the equilibrium price of sterling rises. This could be caused by a
   A   devaluation of the pound.
   B   devaluation of the U.S. dollar.
   C   higher rate of inflation in the U.K. than in the U.S.A.
   D   change in tastes in the U.K. favouring American goods.
   E   change in tastes in the U.S.A. favouring British goods.

5   Assume again the initial equilibrium with demand and supply D^0D^0, S^0S^0.
Britain's trading position in the U.S.A. deteriorates because of the entry
of the Japanese into the American market. At the same time, the British
government fulfils various contracts to buy large amounts of American
military equipment. The effects of the changes are represented in the
diagram. The new equilibrium price of sterling will be

A $3.00
B $2.50
C $2.00
D $1.50
E $1.00

6   The table below gives the visible exports and imports of a country.

	exports		imports	
	price per unit	number of units	price per unit	number of units
year 1	$200	5000	$250	7000
year 2	$280	5000	$300	7000

What has happened to the balance of trade and the terms of trade from
year 1 to year 2?

	balance of trade	terms of trade
A	improved	improved
B	improved	deteriorated
C	deteriorated	improved
D	deteriorated	deteriorated
E	deteriorated	unchanged

7

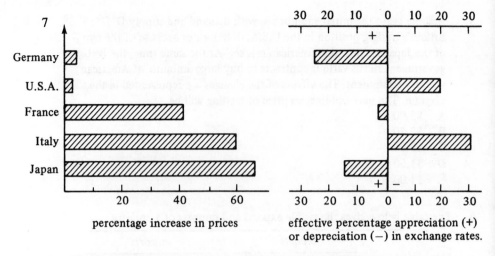

percentage increase in prices

effective percentage appreciation (+) or depreciation (−) in exchange rates.

On the basis of the above data, which relate to a given four-year period, and assuming all countries have the same price elasticity of demand for their exports, which one is most likely to have found *increased* difficulty in exporting?

A   Germany
B   U.S.A.
C   France
D   Italy
E   Japan

8   Any inflationary effects from an increase in the balance of payments surplus can be offset by

A   raising interest rates to check expansion.
B   cutting down on demand for foreign exchange.
C   reducing the exchange rate.
D   lowering domestic price levels.
E   cutting income tax rates.

9   Under a system of fixed exchange rates, exchange margins are the limits within which an exchange rate may move

A   before gold flows in or out.
B   before devaluation or revaluation becomes necessary.
C   in the forward market.
D   before speculation can be profitable.
E   on either side of its par value.

10   Two countries P and Q are each capable of producing at constant cost
     two commodities X and Y. If each country employs one unit of resources on
     each commodity the resulting annual output is

	good X	good Y
country P	40	20
country Q	30	10

If each country employs two units of resources in the production of the commodity for which it has a comparative advantage, and P exchanges a quarter of
its output for Q's output in the ratio $5\,X = 2\,Y$, what is the net gain to Q
(ignoring transport costs)?

A $+10\,X$
B $+\ 5\,X$
C $+15\,Y$
D $+10\,Y$
E $+2.5\,Y$

Exercise 16   The role of the government (1)

1   A public good is one which is supplied
    A   by charity to the needy.
    B   by the nationalised industries.
    C   to all consumers irrespective of whether they pay for it.
    D   to all taxpayers but not to non-taxpayers.
    E   at no opportunity cost.

2   A firm's private costs of production are not equal to the social costs of
    its production.The government could increase economic welfare by
    A   taxing the firm if its social costs exceed its private costs.
    B   taxing the firm if its social costs are less than its private costs.
    C   subsidising the firm if its social costs exceed its private costs.
    D   taxing other firms if social costs exceed private costs in the firm in
        question.
    E   subsidising other firms if social costs are less than private costs in the
        firm in question.

3 Which one of the following policies is most likely to **reduce** the level of structural unemployment?
   A reducing the level of the minimum lending rate
   B increasing labour mobility
   C increasing rates of unemployment benefit
   D reducing income tax and corporation tax rates
   E making increased investment grants available to all companies

4 To stimulate demand in an advanced industrial economy, it would be appropriate for a government to
   A reduce road building.
   B cut grants and subsidies to industry.
   C budget for a surplus.
   D cut taxes.
   E encourage saving.

5 A government could deal with the problems of demand inflation and balance of payment deficit by
   A subsidising exports and reducing taxation.
   B increasing taxation and increasing interest rates.
   C imposing import quotas and reducing interest rates.
   D devaluing the currency and reducing interest rates.
   E devaluing the currency and reducing taxation.

6 A payroll tax imposed on a competitive industry cuts the proportion of labour to capital employed there. This shows that
   A firms are producing under diminishing returns.
   B firms are faced with inelastic demand for their products.
   C firms have been earning supernormal profits.
   D labour and capital are not perfect complements in production.
   E the average rate of return on capital is increasing.

7 Which one of the following measures, which a government might introduce, is most likely to reduce the cost of home ownership?
   A a reduction in interest rates
   B the introduction of a tax on land
   C the diversification of industry
   D a reduction in income tax rates
   E an increase in unemployment benefits

8 Which one of the following taxes is **least** likely to be effective in redistributing inherited wealth?

A   income tax
B   capital gains tax
C   a tax on corporate profits
D   death duties
E   a tax on food

9   Which one of the following taxes is most likely to affect the supply of labour?
A   income tax
B   capital gains tax
C   a tax on coporate profits
D   death duties
E   a tax on food

10   Which one of the following possible consequences of the formation of a monopoly is **not** a cause for government concern?
A   an increase in prices
B   a reduction in the rate of innovation
C   the creation of redundancy
D   the exploitation of economies of scale
E   a curtailment of consumer choice

Exercise 17   The role of the government (2)

1   In which one of the following circumstances is an increase in social welfare payments financed by long-term borrowing **unlikely** to cause prices to rise?
A   a falling average propensity to consume
B   an adverse balance of payments
C   a rising birth rate
D   low interest rates
E   substantial unemployment

2   In a closed economy at full employment, planned saving by households and firms in the coming year is expected to be less than planned investment in the private sector. If the government wishes to maintain full employment, it should
A   reduce investment incentives.
B   increase its own expenditure.
C   aim to reduce its budget surplus or increase its budget deficit.
D   aim to redistribute income from the rich to the poor.
E   cut the rate of corporation tax.

3 Public goods, such as street lighting, are not supplied through the ordinary market mechanism because
   A the initial capital cost would be prohibitive.
   B some households would not be able to afford to make their full contribution towards the cost.
   C the benefits would not be confined to the buyers, but would automatically be available to non-buyers.
   D the provision of public goods is essential, and therefore cannot be left to private initiative.
   E monopolies would earn excess profits.

4 Which one of the following policy measures is likely to be deflationary?
   A an improvement in the foreign exchange rate
   B a reduction in the rate of income tax
   C a reduction in compulsory deposits with the Central Bank
   D an increase in investment allowances
   E an increase in the rate of duty on imported goods

5 As part of a social contract between a government and the trade unions, designed to counter inflation and to run for three years, a 5% norm is set for annual increases in wages and salaries, while domestic prices are to be frozen. If the increase in labour productivity is 2% per annum and the prices of both exports and imports increase by 3% per annum, which one of the following would be expected over the period of the contract?
   A a fall in the real wages of those in employment
   B a rise in the share of profits in the National Income
   C a fall in the number of cash-flow problems experienced by industry
   D a fall in the employment of labour
   E a fall in the desire to export on the part of industry

6 The imposition of rent controls on private rented accommodation at a level below the market rate will tend to
   A lead to an improvement in the quality of the stock of rented accommodation.
   B increase the size of the private rented sector.
   C lengthen the size of the waiting-list for local government houses.
   D improve the prospects for those without houses of finding accommodation.
   E reduce the extent of under-occupation of the existing housing stock.

7   Which one of the following is to be expected as a consequence of the intro-
    duction of government subsidies for shipbuilding?
    A   a decrease in tax receipts
    B   an increase in efficiency amongst producers
    C   an increase in the output of steel
    D   a decrease in interest rates
    E   an unchanged pattern of consumer demand

8   Which one of the following forms of taxation is most regressive?
    A   a poll tax
    B   a flat rate tax on income net of allowances
    C   a proportional income tax
    D   a progressive income tax
    E   a flat rate value-added tax

9   Cost Benefit Analysis is most commonly used in planning
    A   a man-power budget.
    B   a national budget.
    C   the ratio of labour to capital in a productive process.
    D   improvements in industrial relations on the factory floor.
    E   public sector investment projects.

10 In order to use its resources efficiently, a city's passenger transport under-
    taking should charge
    A   higher fares during peak periods because much of the equipment needed
        for peak-period travel is idle for the rest of the day.
    B   lower fares during peak periods to keep down travel costs for the maxi-
        mum number of people.
    C   higher fares during off-peak periods because the cost per passenger
        is higher during these periods.
    D   the same fares throughout the day to avoid distorting people's pre-
        ferences between peak and off-peak travel.
    E   lower fares in the evening during non-working hours when demand
        is likely to be more inelastic.

Test 1 Microeconomics

1 Which one of the following statements is necessarily true of any centrally planned economy?
   A It cannot overcome the problem of economic scarcity, because it cannot use increases in the money supply to finance government expenditure.
   B It cannot overcome the problem of economic scarcity, because it will come up against the constraint of factor limitation.
   C It can overcome the problem of economic scarcity by deciding what is to be produced, thus relieving the consumer of the problem of choice.
   D It can overcome the problem of economic scarcity by income redistribution from rich to poor.
   E It can overcome the problem of scarcity by regulating the price mechanism.

2 Opportunity cost is
   A the price of a close substitute for a certain article.
   B the amount a person would be willing to spend rather than be deprived of a certain good.
   C the amount a person would be willing to risk on an uncertain outcome.
   D the amount of the best alternative good foregone in favour of a purchase.
   E the cost of an investment project.

3 Which one of the following propositions relating to the U.K. economy depends on a value judgement?
   A A reduction in the balance of payments deficit can only be attained at the expense of an increase in the level of unemployment.
   B In the 1960s the government placed too much emphasis on the attainment of equilibrium in the balance of payments at the expense of other policy objectives.
   C The introduction of flexible exchange rates makes it possible to reconcile the external balance of the economy with the pursuit of domestic policy objectives.
   D Flexible exchange rates cannot be relied upon to rectify a balance of payments deficit.
   E The introduction of flexible exchange rates has added to the problem of controlling inflation.

4   If the allocation of resources in a fully employed economy becomes more
    efficient then
    A   the level of real income per head will rise.
    B   income per head will be more equitably distributed.
    C   income per head cannot rise, because of full employment.
    D   producers will gain at the expense of consumers.
    E   there will be unemployed resources.

5   The production possibility curve for an economy producing goods X and
    Y is shown as MN in the diagram below.

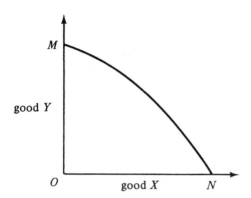

    The curve depicts
    A   the various combinations of X and Y between which the community
        is indifferent.
    B   the relationship between the total resources devoted to the production
        of X and Y respectively.
    C   the amount of X that consumers are prepared to give up in order to
        obtain more of Y at each level of output.
    D   the largest attainable output of Y for any output of X, given existing
        technology and resources.
    E   the benefits to be gained from specialisation in production of either
        X or Y.

6   For a consumer to be in a position of equilibrium it is necessary that his
    A   marginal utility from all goods should be the same.
    B   marginal utility from a $ spent on any good should be the same.
    C   marginal utility from each good should be maximised.
    D   total utility from each good should be the same.
    E   total utility from an expensive good should be greater than that from
        a cheap good.

7   Which one of the following graphs refers to a good which exhibits a positive income elasticity of demand at all levels of income?

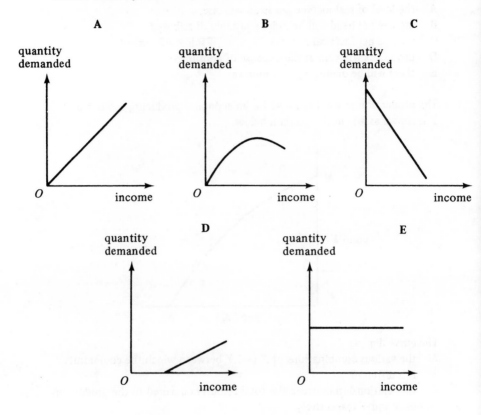

8   If the demand curve for a commodity is a downward-sloping straight line, the elasticity of demand for the commodity, defined as a positive number,
A   is unity.
B   is infinity.
C   decreases as quantity increases.
D   increases as quantity increases.
E   is constant and less than one.

9   An individual is given a voucher worth £3 to spend in a sea-food bar which sells only prawns and oysters. His marginal utility schedules for portions of both foods are given below.

number of portions	marginal utility of prawns	marginal utility of oysters
1	100	160
2	90	150
3	80	140
4	70	130
5	60	120
6	50	110
7	40	100
8	30	90
9	20	80
10	10	70

If the price of a portion of prawns is 15p and that of a portion of oysters is 30p, which combination of portions yields the greatest utility?

	portions of prawns	portions of oysters
A	0	10
B	2	9
C	4	8
D	6	7
E	8	6

10 In the case of a Giffen good, the income effect is in the
   A   opposite direction to the substitution effect and weaker.
   B   opposite direction to the substitution effect and stronger.
   C   opposite direction to the substitution effect and equal in strength.
   D   same direction as the substitution effect and weaker.
   E   same direction as the substitution effect and stronger.

11 The demand function for good A is written as follows:

$$Q_D = 300 - 3P_A + 2P_B - 0.2Y$$

where Q_D is the quantity demanded of good A in millions of tonnes,
$\quad P_A$ is the price of good A in dollars,
$\quad P_B$ is the price of good B in dollars,
$\quad Y$ is the level of national income in millions of dollars.

Initially, when $P_A = 10$, $P_B = 15$ and $Y = 500$, the demand for A is 200. If Y increases to 1000 what is the income elasticity of demand?

A $\quad -\frac{1}{10}$
B $\quad -\frac{1}{5}$
C $\quad -\frac{1}{2}$
D $\quad -1$
E $\quad -2$

12 'If the price of a good is reduced enough to permit a 5 per cent larger quantity to be sold, the total expenditure on the product remains the same.'
   The implication of the above statement is that elasticity of demand with respect to price is
A zero.
B less than one, but not zero.
C equal to one.
D greater than one but less than infinity.
E infinity.

13 If, when the 100% *ad valorem* tax on a commodity is doubled, the tax revenue doubles, the price elasticity of demand for the commodity must be
A 0
B 0.5
C 1.0
D 2.0
E 4.0

14 Assume that the cross elasticity of demand for cars with respect to changes in the price of petrol is $- 0.5$. At an average price per car of £5000, the number of cars sold per week is 10 000. If the average price of cars remains unchanged, but the price of petrol increases from 40p to 44p per litre, the number of cars sold per week will fall to

A   5000
B   7500
C   8500
D   9000
E   9500

15   The demand for butter is negatively related to the price of butter:

$$\text{elasticity} = -0.43$$

The demand for butter is also affected by the prices of flour, margarine, cakes and meat. Cross elasticities of demand for butter with respect to the prices of these goods are:

flour	-0.23
margarine	0.10
cakes	0.59
meat	0.56

Which one of the following can be predicted from this information?
A   A rise in the price of flour will lead to a rise in the demand for butter.
B   A fall in the price of margarine will lead to a rise in the demand for butter.
C   A fall in the price of cakes will lead to a rise in the demand for butter.
D   A fall in the price of meat will lead to a fall in the demand for butter.
E   A fall in the price of butter will lead to a more than proportionate rise in the demand for butter.

16   When marginal production costs are equal to average production costs, then
A   marginal costs are constant.
B   average costs are falling.
C   average costs are at their minimum point.
D   marginal costs are at their minimum point.
E   average fixed costs are constant.

17   Where the prices of factor inputs are constant and a firm can achieve constant returns to scale in production, it follows that
A   the firm's profit tends towards zero in the long run.
B   the long-run marginal cost is falling.
C   the long-run elasticity of supply is equal to one.
D   the long-run average cost of output is constant.
E   total costs rise more slowly than output, in percentage terms.

18   A public utility makes use of a two-part tariff which comprises a substantial fixed standard charge plus a lower charge per unit consumed. Which one of the following diagrams correctly depicts the average cost (*AC*) and marginal cost (*MC*) to the consumer?

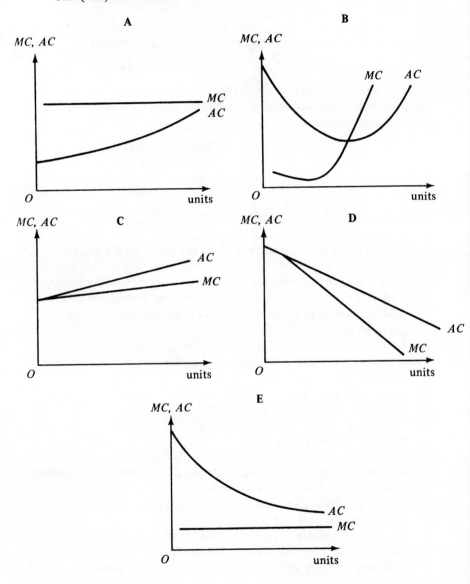

19   If the elasticity of the supply of butter is 0.25 a decrease in its guaranteed
price to farmers from £10 to £9 per tonne will decrease the quantity pro-
duced per week from 1000 tonnes to
A   250 tonnes.
B   500 tonnes.
C   750 tonnes.
D   900 tonnes.
E   975 tonnes.

20

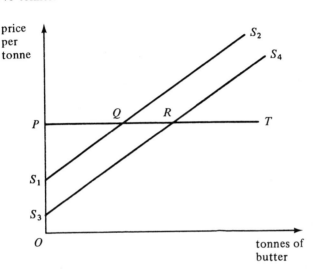

A government decides to prevent the price of butter from rising above *OP*
per tonne, by selling from its substantial stockpile whenever the market
price reaches this level. If the original supply curve was S_1S_2, what will
be the new market supply curve given such intervention?
A   *PQT*
B S_1QT
C S_3RS_4
D S_3RT
E PRS_4

21 The following two sets of information are available about the inputs and outputs of a firm.

	number of men	number of machines	units of total output
I	1	1	30
	2	1	55
	3	1	75
	4	1	90
	5	1	100
II	1	1	30
	2	2	65
	3	3	105
	4	4	150
	5	5	200

Which one of the following statements describes the situation in the firm?
A There are diminishing returns to factors and constant returns to scale.
B There are diminishing returns to factors and increasing returns to scale.
C There are constant returns to factors and diminishing returns to scale.
D There are increasing returns to factors and increasing returns to scale.
E There are increasing returns to factors and decreasing returns to scale.

22 A manufacturer produces two products, X and Y. Market prices of both products go up by the same percentage and his supply of X is increased by 100%, and that of Y by 50%. What can deduced about the elasticity of supply of X and Y?
A The elasticity of X is 2, and that of Y is 1.
B The elasticity of X is 1, and that of Y is $\frac{1}{2}$.
C The elasticity of X is between 1 and 2, and that of Y between $\frac{1}{2}$ and 1.
D The elasticity of X is 1, while that of Y cannot be determined.
E Neither of the elasticities can be determined.

23 Which one of the diagrams below illustrates a supply curve of unit elasticity?

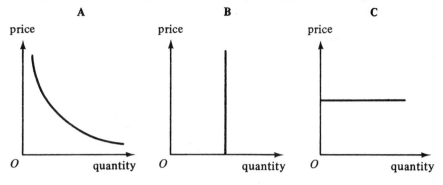

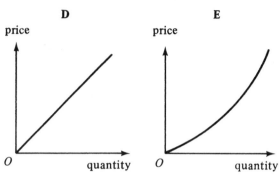

24 If a firm produces under constant returns to scale
   A changes in the quantity produced are determined by the productivity of the variable input.
   B inputs can only be employed in constant proportions.
   C equal proportional changes in all inputs result in the same proportional change in the quantity produced.
   D output remains constant as inputs are increased.
   E a proportional change in any input results in the same proportional change in the quantity produced.

25 A builder owning a plot of land receives permission to build 8 or 9 houses If he builds 8 they will cost $10 000 each and will sell at $12 000. If he builds 9 they will cost $9400 each and will sell at $11 500. The marginal cost of the ninth house is
   A $500
   B $600
   C $1500
   D $2000
   E $4600

26 The diagram illustrates a firm operating under conditions of perfect competition.

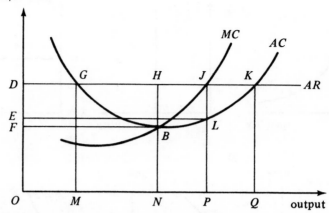

At what level of output will the firm operate in order to maximise its profits?

A *OM*
B *ON*
C *OP*
D *OQ*
E *MQ*

27 The following is known about a firm in long-run equilibrium.

> Average revenue = 15p
> Average cost = 15p
> Marginal cost = 12p
> Marginal revenue = 12p

Which one of the following market forms **cannot** be consistent with this information?

A monopoly
B duopoly
C oligopoly
D monopolistic competition
E perfect competition

28 The following diagram shows the supply and demand curves for tickets for the Football Association Cup Final.

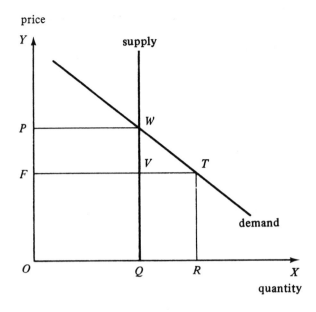

If all tickets are sold at price *OF* rather than the market clearing price, which area in the diagram represents the resultant loss of revenue?

A   *VWT*
B   *FPWV*
C   *FPWT*
D   *QWTR*
E   *QVTR*

29   'Profit-maximisation' implies that the firm will always
     A   produce that quantity of output which can be produced at the lowest average cost.
     B   employ any variable factor up to the point at which the marginal revenue product is equal to its marginal cost.
     C   employ factors of production to maximise the total product.
     D   adopt the most capital-intensive method of production.
     E   cease production if prices falls below average total cost.

30   A firm in a perfectly competitive industry determines
     A   both the price of its product and the quantity it produces.
     B   neither the price of its product nor the quantity it produces.
     C   either the price of its product or the quantity it produces, but not both.
     D   the quantity it produces but not the price of its product.
     E   the price of its product but not the quantity it produces.

31 Which one of the following may be found under conditions of perfect competion?

    A   brand advertising
    B   price discrimination
    C   investment in new plant
    D   market research
    E   differentiated products

32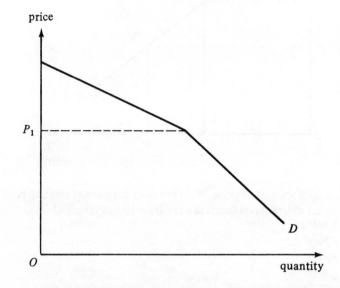

The kinked demand curve above represents market conditions where

    A   the good being demanded is an inferior good.
    B   the income elasticity of demand for a rise in price above P_1 is different from that for a fall in price below P_1.
    C   there is unitary price elasticity at all points on the demand curve.
    D   demand is price inelastic at all points above the kink and price elastic at all points below it.
    E   demand is more price elastic for a rise in price above P_1 than for a fall in price below P_1.

33 Over a period of time the position of the demand curve for a commodity x remains unchanged, yet the price of x falls. This could be explained by

    A   the introduction of a subsidy on consumption of a commodity y which is complementary to x.
    B   an increase in the existing unit tax levied on the output of x.
    C   a reduction in the existing unit tax levied on the output of commodity z which is a substitute for x.

D   the introduction of a subsidy to labourers prepared to work in the industry producing x.

E   a reduction in the supply of capital equipment available to the industry producing x.

34   A firm's total costs for various levels of outputs are given in the table below.

units of output	1	2	3	4	5	6	7	8	9	10
total cost (pence)	7	13	18	22	25	29	34	40	47	55

If the market price were 6p, which one of the following ranges of output would a profit-maximising firm, operating under conditions of perfect competition, choose to produce?

A   1-2
B   3-4
C   5-6
D   7-8
E   9-10

35   Assuming the price elasticity of supply to be greater than the price elasticity of demand, which one of the following would result from an increase in a subsidy on the retail price of milk?

A   Consumers' expenditure would be unaffected.
B   The volume of milk sales would decline.
C   The price of milk to consumers would fall by less than half the extra subsidy per pint.
D   The price of milk to consumers would fall by more than half the extra subsidy per pint.
E   Producers' profits would increase to the full extent of the subsidy.

36   Mr Smith possesses skills which allow him a choice among three jobs, X, Y and Z, whose wages are shown below. He is equally interested in all three jobs and chooses among them solely on the basis of the wages offered.

job	X	Y	Z
wage	$60	$50	$35

If Mr Smith chooses X, his transfer earnings must be

A $60 because this is the reward offered by the job of his choice.
B $60 because this is the highest wage offered by any of the alternatives.
C $50 because he is only prepared to choose X if the wage offered is at least equal to $50.
D $50 because this represents the middle of the range of opportunities.
E $35 because this is the lowest wage offered if he rejects X and Y.

37 The normal profit of a firm is defined as
   A   that profit needed to keep the firm in equilibrium.
   B   the average profit it earns over a period of years.
   C   the level of profit sufficient to cover capital depreciation.
   D   that profit earned where marginal cost equals marginal revenue.
   E   that profit needed in the long run to keep its resources in their present use.

38 A firm operates under perfect competition in both product and factor markets with labour as the only variable input. In the diagram below, the line PQ shows the relation between the marginal physical product of labour and the man-hours hired.

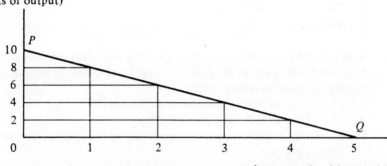

marginal physical
product of labour
(units of output)

man-hours per day (thousands)

When the wage rate is £3 per man-hour the firm finds that it maximises profits by employing 3000 man-hours per day.

At what price is the firm's final product sold in the market?
   A   £0.25
   B   £0.75
   C   £9.00
   D   £12.00
   E   £24.00

39 The economic rent earned by a unit of a factor of production is the difference between its market price and its
   A   average cost.
   B   marginal cost.
   C   replacement cost.
   D   opportunity cost.
   E   historical cost.

40   A trade union obtains a wage settlement which raises the level of wages of
     a certain section of its workers above their estimated marginal revenue
     product. Which one of the following is the most likely effect of this?
     A   More men will be employed because the higher wage rate attracts them.
     B   The firm will increase its output to pay the increased wage bill.
     C   The firm will not replace some of the men who retire or move off to
         other jobs.
     D   Employers, anxious to keep down unit costs, will be dissuaded from
         taking on more capital equipment.
     E   The marginal revenue productivity of the workers will immediately
         rise to the level of the higher wage rate, without any fall in the number
         employed.

Test 2   Macroeconomics

1   'Transfer Income' is income
    A   for which no corresponding good or service is exchanged.
    B   taxed by the government.
    C   received from investment of capital.
    D   received from overseas trade.
    E   in the form of surpluses of public corporations.

2   A director becomes redundant as a result of a company merger. His salary
    in employment was £10 000 per annum. He is entitled to a redundancy
    payment of £5000 (£4000 as a lump sum and £1000 as 10% of his salary).
    His wife takes up employment at a wage of £1000 per annum and his
    daughter increases the contribution to the family housekeeping by £500
    from her earnings.
    The net reduction in the contribution of the family to the measured National
    Income in the first year of the father's redundancy is
    A   £5000
    B   £6500
    C   £7500
    D   £8500
    E   £9000

3   A firm's income and expenditure in a particular year were as follows.

Expenditure		Income	
	£thousands		£thousands
wage costs	200	revenue from sales of	
rent and interest		final products	800
payments	100	revenue from sales of	
raw materials costs	600	by-products	200
total expenditure =	900	total revenue =	1000

	£thousands
surplus	100
depreciation of capital	50
net profit over the year	50

Net value added by this firm was
A   £1 000 000
B   £ 450 000
C   £ 350 000
D   £ 200 000
E   £   50 000

4   Consider the following data from the National Income Accounts of a country whose net property income from abroad is zero.

Item	$m
Total domestic expenditure at market prices	100 000
Exports of goods and services	20 000
Imports of goods and services	25 000
Taxes on expenditure	9000
Subsidies	500

The value of the Gross National Product at factor cost is
A $66 500m.
B $83 500m.
C $86 500m.
D $91 500m.
E $103 500m.

5   The national income of a country can be estimated by calculating the
    A   total of all personal incomes.
    B   total of all factor incomes.
    C   profits of business enterprises.
    D   surplus of government current revenue over current expenditure.
    E   surplus on the balance of payments on current account.

6   Which one of the following will lead to an increase in the level of economic
    activity within an economy?
    A   a decrease in exports
    B   a fall in domestic investment
    C   a rise in the propensity to save
    D   a fall in bank lending
    E   a fall in the budget surplus

7   If, in a closed economy with no public sector, the value of the investment
    multiplier falls, which one of the following statements must be true?
    A   The marginal propensity to consume has fallen.
    B   The average propensity to consume has fallen.
    C   Planned investment has fallen.
    D   Liquidity preference has fallen.
    E   The economy is in a state of disequilibrium.

8   The National Income of a simple economy, in which there is neither govern-
    ment economic activity nor foreign trade, is in equilibrium at £30 000m. Its
    full employment National Product is £35 000m and the marginal propensity
    to consume is four-fifths. How large an injection of investment is required
    to bring the economy into equilibrium at full employment?
    A   £500m
    B   £1000m
    C   £2000m
    D   £4000m
    E   £5000m

9   A country experiences an 'Inflationary Gap' when
    A   the value of its exports is less than the value of its imports.
    B   there is a budget surplus.
    C   real income differentials widen during a period of rising prices.
    D   it experiences price increases that are larger than those of its competitors.
    E   aggregate demand in real terms is greater than the full employment
         level of output.

10 In the following, C = Consumption, S = Saving, Y = Income, and b is the marginal propensity to consume. In a closed economy with no government sector, and where investment is given, the consumption function is $C = 50 + bY$. The multiplier is 5. It may be inferred that

A $S = 50 + 0.8Y$
B $C = 50 + 0.5Y$
C $C = 50 + 0.8Y$
D $S = 50 + 0.2Y$
E $C = 50 + 0.2Y$

11

disposable family income (£)	consumption expenditure (£)	saving (£)
2000	2150	− 150
3000	3100	− 100
4000	4000	0
5000	4850	150
6000	5650	350
7000	6380	620

Throughout the range of disposable incomes shown in the table above, as income rises the average propensity to consume

A remains constant.
B goes down and then rises.
C falls continuously.
D rises continuously.
E rises and then goes down.

12 In an economy with a government sector but no foreign trade sector, the level of National Income will be that which results in which one of the following equalities?

A $S = I$
B $T^i = G$
C $T^d - G = I - S$
D $T^i + T^d = D + G$
E $S + T^i + T^d = I + D + G$

(S = Savings, I = Investment, G = Government expenditure on goods/services, T^i = Indirect taxes, T^d = Direct taxes, D = Subsidies)

13 Which one of the following items constitutes a leakage from the circular flow of income of an economy?

A   the purchase of a domestically produced good by a domestic company
B   the purchase of a domestically produced good by a foreign company
C   the payment of value-added tax on goods sold in the domestic market
D   government aid to companies in financial difficulties
E   benefits paid by the government to redundant workers

14   The diagram below represents the functions for total expenditure (*E*),
injections (*J*) and leakages (*W*) in an economy in which *OY* is the full employment level of income.

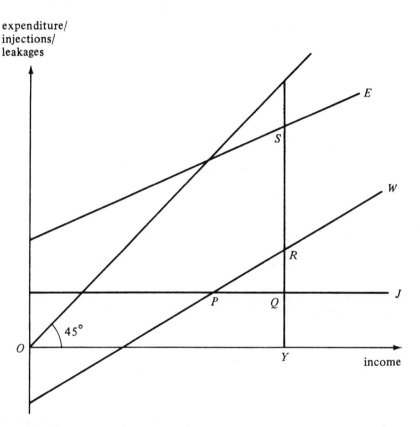

Which one of the following is a measure of the deflationary gap?
A   *PQ*
B   *YR*
C   *QR*
D   *RS*
E   *QY–RQ*

15 Which one of the following is an example of monetary policy?
  A the creation of a budget surplus
  B a prices and incomes policy
  C a demand for special deposits
  D the suspension of investment allowances for industry
  E the introduction of a wealth tax

16 Assume that the banking sector maintains a 10% reserve assets ratio and that the non-bank private sector has a fixed demand for cash. An initial increase by £1 in both reserves and deposits of the banking system will permit an ultimate increase in the deposits of the banking system of
  A £0.10
  B £0.90
  C £1.00
  D £5.00
  E £10.00

17 Changes are made in the 'weights' used in a retail price index mainly to
  A prevent the increase in prices from appearing too inflationary.
  B take advantage of the latest data gathering techniques.
  C allow for quality changes which have taken place in commodities.
  D achieve greater conformity between the index and current consumer spending patterns.
  E make the base point consistent with other official indices.

18 Which one of the following actions by a central bank would reduce the supply of money in a country?
  A buying securities on the open market
  B requesting commercial banks to increase advances
  C requiring the commerical banks to lower special deposits at the central bank
  D increasing the minimum liquidity requirements of the commercial banks
  E lowering the Bank Rate (minimum lending rate)

19 A bond matures in one year, at which time the holder will receive its maturity value of £100 plus annual interest of £10. If the present-day market value of the bond is £98, the market rate of interest is
  A approximately 12%.
  B 10%.
  C 9.8%.
  D approximately 2%.
  E not calculable from the information given.

20   A person's income increases from $100 to $120 per week. At the same time
     the general price level rises from 100 to 130, entirely because taxes on
     cigarettes and alcoholic drinks have doubled. If the person concerned does
     not smoke or drink, he has had a
     A   rise in both his money income and his real income.
     B   rise in his money income but a fall in his real income.
     C   fall in his money income but a rise in his real income.
     D   fall in both his money income and his real income.
     E   change in his income which is indeterminate.

21   If over a period of time the money supply has increased from £10 000 million
     to £12 000 million and the National Income from £30 000 million to £48 000
     million, the income velocity of circulation of money has risen
     A   by one-fifth.
     B   by one-ninth.
     C   from one-third to one-quarter.
     D   ninefold.
     E   from 3 to 4.

22   In Keynesian theory the 'speculative demand' for money will increase when
     A   interest rates increase.
     B   interest rates decrease.
     C   interest rates remain stable for a long period of time.
     D   the level of money income remains constant for a long period of time.
     E   the transactions demand for money rises.

23   Which one of the following is most likely to see a worsening of his economic
     position during a period of unanticipated inflation?
     A   a fixed income receiver
     B   a debtor
     C   an equity shareholder
     D   an importer
     E   an entrepreneur

24   What conditions must be fulfilled before the Quantity Theory of Money can be
     used to predict the price level?
     A   falling income velocity of money and full employment
     B   constant income velocity of money and full employment
     C   rising income velocity of money and full employment
     D   rising income velocity of money and rising employment
     E   constant income velocity of money and falling employment

25   The rate of exchange, officially, between £ in country A and $ in country B
     is $2.40 = £1. To be as well off in country B, a citizen of country A earning
     £800 per year requires to earn $2400 per year in country B. What is the
     'purchasing power parity' between the £ and the $?
     A   7.2:1
     B   3.0:1
     C   2.4:1
     D   1.0:1
     E   0.8:1

26   Which one of the following by itself is most likely to increase international
     demand for German marks?
     A   a fall in rates of interest in Germany
     B   an increase in the rate of inflation in Germany
     C   an increase in the productivity of labour in other countries competing
         against German industrial goods
     D   expectations of a devaluation of the dollar and of the pound sterling
     E   poor summer weather in German tourist areas

27   A British doll manufacturer sets his prices in pounds sterling and sells 90
     dolls per week in the U.S.A. when the price is £2 per doll and the exchange
     rate is £1 = $2. The demand curve for his product in the U.S.A. has unit
     price elasticity. Assuming an unchanged sterling price, what is the maximum
     number of dolls per week he can sell if the exchange rate changes to £1 =
     $1.5?
     A   60
     B   90
     C   120
     D   135
     E   150

28   What is meant by a surplus in the current account of the balance of pay-
     ments?
     A   an excess of gold and capital received over gold and capital paid abroad
     B   an excess of total debits over total credits in the balance of payments
     C   an excess value of export goods over import goods
     D   an excess value of exported services over imported services
     E   an excess of total receipts from goods and services over total payments
         for goods and services, plus net interest payments from overseas

29 The table shows the number of man-days taken to produce an equivalent amount of each of six commodities in each of two countries X and Y.

	coal	cotton	wool	iron	wheat	maize
country X	120	60	70	100	140	80
country Y	100	25	35	90	90	20

Assuming there are no other costs of production, which two commodities is country Y most likely to import from country X?

A   coal and iron
B   coal and wheat
C   cotton and maize
D   cotton and wool
E   wheat and maize

30 If, in response to a devaluation of a country's currency by 20%, the quantity of a good imported into the country falls from 200 000 tonnes to 190 000 tonnes, the price elasticity of demand for the good is approximately

A   0.10
B   0.125
C   0.25
D   0.40
E   0.50

31 There is an increased likelihood that a country with a fixed exchange rate will suffer a fall in its reserves of foreign currency if it experiences

A   an increase in merchandise exports.
B   a reduction in invisible imports.
C   an increase in long-term investment abroad.
D   a reduction in transfer payments to non-residents.
E   an increase in short-term liabilities to non-residents.

32 If the U.K. has a freely fluctuating exchange rate, the price of foreign currencies (in terms of pounds) will tend to rise when

A   U.K. overseas military expenditures are reduced.
B   U.K. tourists spend more abroad.
C   Germans switch their purchases from Volkswagens to British Leyland.
D   U.K. residents switch their purchases from Volkswagens to British Leyland.
E   U.K. aid to foreign countries is reduced.

33 Fiscal policy attempts to regulate the economy by varying
   A the level of the rate of interest.
   B the quantity of money in circulation.
   C the velocity of circulation of money.
   D the structure of the National Debt.
   E the level of government expenditure.

34 To reduce demand in an advanced industrial economy, it would be appropriate for a government to
   A change the balance of taxation in favour of progressive taxes.
   B reduce taxation.
   C increase investment allowances to industry.
   D discourage saving.
   E budget for a surplus.

35 During a recession, a government may raise the level of employment by
   A budgeting for a deficit and borrowing in order to fill the gap.
   B budgeting for a surplus so as to have extra funds for distribution.
   C making large-scale reductions in public expenditure, so as to encourage private-sector investment.
   D offering better terms on national savings, so as to encourage the private sector to save more.
   E creating forced savings by fiscal means in order to pay off debt.

36 The effect on a country's trade of a change in the comparative value of its currency depends upon the elasticity of supply of, and demand for, its imports and exports. In which one of the following cases would a country derive the greatest benefit in its balance of trade from a fall in the value of its currency?

	demand for imports	demand for exports	supply of imports	supply of exports
A	elastic	inelastic	elastic	elastic
B	elastic	elastic	elastic	elastic
C	elastic	elastic	inelastic	inelastic
D	elastic	inelastic	inelastic	elastic
E	inelastic	elastic	elastic	inelastic

37 If a government wishes to maintain full employment without excess demand and, at the same time, reduce direct taxation, it should
   A adopt a restrictive monetary policy.
   B devalue the currency.
   C impose import controls.
   D increase subsidies to nationalised industries.
   E provide additional incentives for private investment and house building.

38   Government policy results in an increase in a country's National Debt. The
       suggestion that the additional interest payments constitute a future claim
       on the country's resources is true if
       A   part of all of the debt is incurred overseas.
       B   there is unemployment which the government is trying to reduce.
       C   interest rates are rising.
       D   the debt incurred is long-term rather than short-term.
       E   interest paid on government bonds is not subject to income tax.

39   When National Income equals £50 000 million and government spending
       equals £15 000 million, an economy is in equilibrium. Out of every increase
       of £100 in National Income, £5 is taken in taxes, £15 is spent on imports
       and £20 is saved. To raise National Income to a full employment level of
       £60 000 million the government will need to raise its own spending to
       A   £16000 million.
       B   £19000 million.
       C   £25000 million.
       D   £28000 million.
       E   £30000 million.

40   The table below provides hypothetical data on National Income and domestic
       expenditure for three years.

	year 1 (£m)	year 2 (£m)	year 3 (£m)
National Income	200	220	240
consumer spending	120	120	130
government spending	60	60	60
investment	40	40	40

       In which year(s) will the government be faced with a balance of payments
       deficit?
       A   1 and 3
       B   2 and 3
       C   1 only
       D   2 only
       E   3 only

Item statistics and correct answers

For every multiple choice item in this book, the performance of the examination candidates has been analysed to provide a facility value and a discrimination index. These statistics, along with the correct options, are presented in the tables which follow.

The *facility value* of an item is the percentage of candidates who responded correctly (no mark is awarded to any candidate who chooses more than one option). The item's *discrimination index* is the (point-biserial) correlation[1] between success in responding to the item and score on the examination mutiple choice test of which it was a part. Thus an item's discrimination index tends to be high when all those who do well on a **test** respond correctly to the item and when all those who do badly respond incorrectly or not at all. The maximum possible discrimination index is +1 and most of the items in the Advanced Level Economics examinations are intended to have discrimination indices greater than 0.25.

The average facility, and thus the average score of examination candidates on the items in this book, is approximately 54%. Of course, since A-level courses differ in content and emphasis, certain items will be less valid as tests of one course than of others, and teachers should bear this in mind, both in setting exercises for their students and in interpreting the results.

In the table following there will be found, under each item number, the letter for the correct option, the item's facility value and the item's discrimination index.

[1] The point-biserial correlation (r) is calculated as follows:

$$r = \frac{M_g - M_t}{\sigma_t} \left(\sqrt{\frac{p}{q}} \right)$$

where M_g = the mean total score on the test of the group choosing the correct option.
M_t = the mean total score on the test of the total sample.
p = the proportion of candidates choosing the correct option.
q = the proportion of candidates not choosing the correct option.
σ_t = the standard deviation of the total test score in the complete sample.

1.1	1.2	1.3	1.4	1.5	1.6	1.7	1.8	1.9	1.10
A	D	D	B	C	E	C	A	E	E
90%	82%	56%	40%	61%	74%	24%	74%	70%	63%
0.15	0.29	0.20	0.35	0.33	0.24	0.28	0.33	0.37	0.28

2.1	2.2	2.3	2.4	2.5	2.6	2.7	2.8	2.9	2.10
D	E	C	B	C	E	A	D	D	A
83%	75%	37%	47%	45%	42%	74%	71%	79%	41%
0.28	0.33	0.30	0.09	0.36	0.40	0.34	0.33	0.27	0.22

3.1	3.2	3.3	3.4	3.5	3.6	3.7	3.8	3.9	3.10
C	D	B	A	A	D	E	B	A	C
78%	33%	71%	52%	46%	46%	31%	49%	39%	62%
0.38	0.38	0.41	0.37	0.31	0.34	0.40	0.38	0.20	0.39

4.1	4.2	4.3	4.4	4.5	4.6	4.7	4.8	4.9	4.10
D	B	D	E	A	B	C	E	E	C
77%	62%	58%	52%	59%	41%	61%	59%	67%	67%
0.38	0.27	0.40	0.34	0.34	0.35	0.36	0.27	0.31	0.49

5.1	5.2	5.3	5.4	5.5	5.6	5.7	5.8	5.9	5.10
D	A	B	D	C	D	C	D	D	E
68%	45%	41%	32%	36%	45%	82%	46%	68%	19%
0.27	0.22	0.22	0.38	0.18	0.37	0.39	0.20	0.47	0.35

6.1	6.2	6.3	6.4	6.5	6.6	6.7	6.8	6.9	6.10
B	D	C	D	C	A	D	C	B	A
86%	60%	76%	63%	63%	54%	54%	51%	52%	69%
0.36	0.26	0.42	0.45	0.11	0.44	0.28	0.33	0.32	0.34

7.1	7.2	7.3	7.4	7.5	7.6	7.7	7.8	7.9	7.10
E	E	C	C	A	C	E	B	B	A
64%	50%	63%	86%	80%	73%	20%	48%	27%	54%
0.36	0.28	0.30	0.33	0.29	0.24	0.34	0.36	0.37	0.38

8.1	8.2	8.3	8.4	8.5	8.6	8.7	8.8	8.9	8.10
D	A	B	B	D	C	B	E	B	B
53%	67%	52%	83%	63%	79%	52%	40%	48%	47%
0.38	0.26	0.44	0.11	0.32	0.36	0.40	0.16	0.29	0.29

9.1	9.2	9.3	9.4	9.5	9.6	9.7	9.8	9.9	9.10
B	C	E	A	A	A	E	E	A	E
59%	83%	35%	55%	31%	42%	62%	69%	70%	79%
0.42	0.19	0.25	0.45	0.23	0.22	0.49	0.35	0.32	0.29

10.1	10.2	10.3	10.4	10.5	10.6	10.7	10.8	10.9	10.10
E	B	C	C	B	D	A	D	C	C
33%	65%	52%	38%	59%	70%	58%	57%	47%	44%
0.20	0.33	0.35	0.25	0.35	0.45	0.41	0.44	0.25	0.51

11.1	11.2	11.3	11.4	11.5	11.6	11.7	11.8	11.9	11.10
B	C	A	A	C	B	C	A	C	B
30%	30%	45%	58%	53%	34%	66%	68%	24%	58%
0.34	0.19	0.24	0.42	0.28	0.26	0.46	0.23	0.35	0.26

12.1	12.2	12.3	12.4	12.5	12.6	12.7	12.8	12.9	12.10
B	E	A	B	C	D	B	B	D	A
63%	64%	63%	53%	59%	55%	49%	47%	83%	60%
0.27	0.44	0.37	0.45	0.44	0.28	0.34	0.35	0.28	0.37

13.1	13.2	13.3	13.4	13.5	13.6	13.7	13.8	13.9	13.10
C	A	E	A	A	C	C	D	B	A
68%	32%	58%	45%	59%	49%	60%	42%	47%	45%
0.32	0.31	0.44	0.49	0.45	0.33	0.40	0.32	0.28	0.20

14.1	14.2	14.3	14.4	14.5	14.6	14.7	14.8	14.9	14.10
D	B	B	A	B	E	E	B	D	B
55%	65%	36%	71%	64%	31%	61%	62%	27%	39%
0.26	0.35	0.20	0.41	0.39	0.34	0.41	0.27	0.18	0.20

15.1	15.2	15.3	15.4	15.5	15.6	15.7	15.8	15.9	15.10
E	B	B	E	E	A	E	A	E	B
47%	29%	51%	51%	40%	50%	33%	45%	55%	50%
0.40	0.35	0.26	0.45	0.41	0.23	0.31	0.21	0.30	0.41

16.1	16.2	16.3	16.4	16.5	16.6	16.7	16.8	16.9	16.10
C	A	B	D	B	D	A	E	A	D
54%	51%	67%	71%	61%	40%	41%	71%	56%	69%
0.23	0.41	0.27	0.40	0.32	0.17	0.31	0.39	0.30	0.40

17.1	17.2	17.3	17.4	17.5	17.6	17.7	17.8	17.9	17.10
E	A	C	A	D	C	C	A	E	A
24%	32%	37%	30%	40%	31%	53%	35%	54%	50%
0.31	0.16	0.24	0.28	0.34	0.32	0.28	0.32	0.35	0.28

T1.1	T1.2	T1.3	T1.4	T1.5	T1.6	T1.7	T1.8	T1.9	T1.10
B	D	B	A	D	B	A	C	D	B
33%	87%	47%	67%	47%	33%	73%	40%	42%	42%
0.19	0.35	0.38	0.31	0.34	0.41	0.32	0.34	0.37	0.25

T1.11	T1.12	T1.13	T1.14	T1.15	T1.16	T1.17	T1.18	T1.19	T1.20
C	C	A	E	D	C	D	E	E	B
43%	58%	56%	67%	28%	72%	57%	27%	59%	53%
0.35	0.47	0.36	0.35	0.46	0.29	0.28	0.33	0.39	0.42

T1.21	T1.22	T1.23	T1.24	T1.25	T1.26	T1.27	T1.28	T1.29	T1.30
B	E	D	C	E	C	E	B	B	D
56%	66%	71%	36%	68%	68%	64%	70%	70%	59%
0.25	0.44	0.25	0.26	0.44	0.49	0.37	0.30	0.39	0.28

T1.31	T1.32	T1.33	T1.34	T1.35	T1.36	T1.37	T1.38	T1.39	T1.40
C	E	D	D	D	C	E	B	D	C
62%	70%	40%	56%	36%	48%	54%	39%	63%	69%
0.40	0.36	0.28	0.33	0.30	0.24	0.42	0.35	0.27	0.35

T2.1	T2.2	T2.3	T2.4	T2.5	T2.6	T2.7	T2.8	T2.9	T2.10
A	E	C	C	B	E	A	B	E	C
78%	42%	15%	54%	68%	44%	45%	59%	70%	45%
0.32	0.45	0.24	0.24	0.26	0.37	0.35	0.49	0.40	0.45

T2.11	T2.12	T2.13	T2.14	T2.15	T2.16	T2.17	T2.18	T2.19	T2.20
C	E	C	C	C	E	D	D	A	A
59%	62%	63%	59%	61%	56%	70%	60%	39%	69%
0.36	0.34	0.43	0.19	0.44	0.43	0.33	0.53	0.32	0.32

T2.21	T2.22	T2.23	T2.24	T2.25	T2.26	T2.27	T2.28	T2.29	T2.30
E	B	A	B	B	D	C	E	A	C
44%	49%	80%	67%	54%	77%	63%	59%	34%	59%
0.45	0.16	0.46	0.37	0.24	0.19	0.31	0.31	0.27	0.50

T2.31	T2.32	T2.33	T2.34	T2.35	T2.36	T2.37	T2.38	T2.39	T2.40
C	B	E	E	A	B	A	A	B	C
54%	67%	49%	47%	51%	38%	48%	46%	46%	68%
0.24	0.30	0.36	0.38	0.49	0.30	0.20	0.35	0.32	0.24